ISSUES OF GLOBALIZATION
Case Studies in Contemporary Anthropology
Series Editors: Carla Freeman and Li Zhang

Marriage After Migration

An Ethnography of Money, Romance, and Gender in Globalizing Mexico

NORA HAENN

New York   Oxford
OXFORD UNIVERSITY PRESS

Oxford University Press is a department of the University of Oxford.
It furthers the University's objective of excellence in research, scholarship,
and education by publishing worldwide. Oxford is a registered trade mark of
Oxford University Press in the UK and certain other countries.

Published in the United States of America by Oxford University Press
198 Madison Avenue, New York, NY 10016, United States of America.

© 2020 by Oxford University Press

For titles covered by Section 112 of the US Higher Education
Opportunity Act, please visit www.oup.com/us/he for the latest
information about pricing and alternate formats.

Library of Congress Cataloging-in-Publication Data

CIP data is on file at the Library of Congress
978-0-19-005601-8

Printing number: 9 8 7 6 5 4 3 2 1
Printed by Sheridan Books, Inc., United States of America

To JSR for teaching me about hosts and guests.
And to all people everywhere who care for someone far from home.

To the children whose lives have been touched by events like those described in this
book, I offer these stories in the hope they bring some clarity.

CONTENTS

ACKNOWLEDGMENTS

Travelers never stop relying on the hospitality of hosts. Indeed, hosts make traveling possible. When I first met people in Calakmul, they were too poor to afford hotels. Restaurants were a wealthy person's place where Calakmuleños might be turned away for their dark skin or their Indigenous heritage. Thus, people said of faraway towns and villages, "I know so-and-so there. *Tengo donde llegar. I have a place to stay there.*" If the maps Calakmuleños carried in their minds could be hung on a wall, there would be pins flagging the homes where family and friends awaited them. Given the number of people who took in me and this book, my own map is thick with pins.

Well before I typed the book's first sentence, Rick Wilk showed me a path where I could not see one for myself. Rick edited multiple drafts of my first book, and I only understood the extent of his guidance when I struggled on this second book without him. In my days as a graduate student, the historian George Alter created an exciting community of population researchers, thereby ensconcing migration in my repertoire. The always gracious Carol Greenhouse quietly observed the absence of women's perspectives in my first book. Her comment burrowed its way into my conscience. Sometimes, we think we are starting out on a journey only to find others had set us on our way long ago.

In Calakmul, I first stayed at the home of the Gomez Santiago family years before contemplating this book. In all, the Gomez Santiago have shared their home with me for a year and a half. Much of the book's material I learned by accompanying the family day in, day out. When I first hung my hammock in their home, Fernando Gomez welcomed me with assurances for my safety, "Here you'll be okay. Nobody will touch you. Nobody will steal your things." In my corner of the United States, we say to our houseguests "make yourself at home" and "feel free to rummage around the kitchen." The customary difference is notable and indicates the concerns Calakmuleños carry with them on their travels.

I have many people in Mexico to thank for keeping me safe and not stealing my things. First, it's worth mentioning the Gomez Santiago family individually. In addition to Fernando Gomez and María Santiago, their children Salvador, Elias, Maribel, Esther, Abigail, Nery, Samuel, Moises, and Rosa, along with Fernando and Maria's daughters-in-law, sons-in-law, and grandchildren, offered first-hand insight into changing family life in Calakmul. Nelly Pérez and Alberto Villaseñor have also been generous with a bed. Nelly's rule is that no guest in her house should have to cook or wash dishes. I would add that visitors to the Villaseñor Pérez family are also guaranteed hilarity and top-notch social analyses. Birgit Schmook, Rene Forster, Sophie Calmé, and Mauro Sanvicente offered landing bases in the city of Chetumal. Chetumal is home to the University of Quintana Roo, where Rene teaches, and ECOSUR, El Colegio de la Frontera Sur, where Birgit and Sophie teach. Thus, in addition to food, lodging, and help with other essential logistics, the Chetumal crowd provided the special kind of nourishment required by researchers, that is, academic community.

It's an anthropological truism that a gift given must be returned in some form. I eagerly await the day the United States is receptive enough to travelers from Mexico that I can promise Fernando, Maria, and the family a safe stay in my own home. I await the day Nelly sits at my kitchen table while I take my turn washing the dishes.

There are more people to thank in Mexico. The short list includes Armando Hernández Gómez, Catalina López Jimenez, the Hernández López family, the Hernández Gómez family, and the López Jimenez family; Abelardo Gómez López, Venancia Gómez López, and the Gómez Gómez family, especially Aureliano Gómez Gómez; Margarito Mendez Martinez, Leticia Lima Joachín, and the Lima Joachín family; Margarita Díaz Méndez; Mauricio López Pérez, Rossemelly Burgos Ávila, Manuela Caamas Tun, and Norma Poot. The long list would approach a census for the county of Calakmul, as over the years hundreds have agreed to interviews and surveys. My ability to carry out these surveys and interviews was aided by the National Science Foundation (BCS1193739, BCS 0957354), a fellowship from Fulbright-García Robles, as well as the good citizens of the United States and Mexico who support these programs and their work in scientific learning and bi-national understanding.

In the United States, this book was also taken in by numerous people, sometimes for the equivalent of a light lunch or a stopover on a very lengthy journey. People who helped with the book's messaging include Lisa Cliggett, Emily Duwel, Roxane Henderson, Fred Holmes, Anne McEnany, Seth Murray, Birgit Schmook, Cynthia Werner, Bill Westermeyer, Matt and Kim Young, and students in NCSU's International Studies capstone courses. To improve the writing, I imposed draft chapters on David Casarett, Risa Ellovich, Hannah Gill, Alyson Harding (who also helped with the literature review), Jessica Price Hernandez, Christie Kimsey, Gento Steve Krieger, Dan Mackinnon, Michelle Moran-Taylor, Marie Navarre, and Chizo Wagner. Claudia Radel's ground-breaking work on gender in Calakmul cleared the way for those of us who follow. Shindo Shahreyar Atiae regularly checked in to see how the trip was going. My mother, Grace Corr Haenn, my siblings, Mary Grace, Nancy, Meg, Christine, Ginny, Trisha, Teresa, Cecilia, Rosemary, and Joe, and my first teachers in transnational family life, Tatiana Melodelgado and José Melodelgado, all gave sustenance of one kind or another that kept the project on the road. I am grateful to each and every one of them.

Others in the United States found that the book was more like a long-term lodger, and possibly one whose drawn-out visit stretched the bounds of hospitality. Molly Mullin (see mollymullin.com) didn't just give the manuscript a developmental edit, she lay awake at night contemplating its journey. Molly is an editor who cares! Colleagues and friends who restocked provisions, shared my anthropological and migration interests, and helped when I needed time away include Troy Case, Martha Crowely, Kim Ebert, Sinikka Elliott, Chelsey Juarez, Bea Kendall, Carol Ann Lewald, Lisa and Denny Meeker, John Millhauser, Seth Murray, and Tim Wallace. Helga Braunbeck, Blair Kelley, and Bill Smith supported me with leave time to make the research and writing possible. Rebecca Dnsitran made sense of the mess and magnificence that are marital relationships. It might sound funny to thank Fred Gould and the whole Genetic Engineering and Society (GES) group at NCSU in a book about international migration, but their support never flagged. With a curious intellect and love for smallholding agriculture, Fred read an earlier draft of the book. The larger GES crowd shows that a comforting stay can be found in any academic community where norms of respectful, egalitarian, and transparent debate prevail.

Writing the book forced me to explore new places on the academic landscape. Debbie Boehm and Michelle Moran-Taylor opened doors and provided key guidance in the field of migration studies. Sasha Newell sent me to pivotal research on witchcraft and the intersection of sex and globalization. When I came to a crossroads with Calakmuleño healing practices, Michelle Rivkin-Fish gave me direction. Lisa Cliggett stood by my side throughout, assuring me I would always have a friend with whom to share tales of my travels.

Two fellow voyagers deserve the largest pins in the map. Without them, I doubt I would have hazarded this trip. Looking back over the travel diary that is my anthropological fieldnotes, I came across a conversation with Madeleine Adelman from a decade ago. That conversation included all the book's central themes. Madeleine's expertise in gender and marriage, her pioneering work on domestic violence, and her intellectual generosity gave this book momentum.

Luis Melodelgado was my trail buddy for much of this project. His presence settled Elvia's and others' concerns regarding my marital status. His playfulness and ability to lighten hearts was a gift to Calakmuleños traumatized by structural violence. Luis carried out key interviews with Calakmuleño men, expanded my understanding of Calakmul's cultural context, and remains an invaluable translator and friend.

Even with all this help, the journey was not quite over. I needed fresh energy to complete the last leg. At Oxford University Press, Brianna McClure, along with Meredith Keffer's confidence in the project, helped transform an unwieldy manuscript into a manageable one. I would also like to thank the following reviewers for their detailed feedback:

Nobuko Adachi, Illinois State University
Michael Chibnik, University of Iowa
Jeffrey H. Cohen, Ohio State University
Chuck Darrah, San Jose State University
Margaret Dorsey, University of Texas, Rio Grande Valley
David McMurray, Oregon State University
Ruth Gomberg-Muñoz, Loyola University Chicago
Jason Pribilsky, Whitman College
5 anonymous reviewers

Margaret Dorsey, in particular, cheered me on with the academic equivalent of "Don't give up now!" Finally, Ed Huddleston, the copy editor with a good eye, championed the manuscript as if it were his own. He read every word twice over and smoothed out the language. Ed took a long, arduous trek over rocky terrain and made it all read like an evening stroll through the neighborhood.

CHAPTER 1

Why Marriage and Migration

Paulita pleaded with her husband not to travel to Alabama. Standing shorter than five feet tall, with the plump figure of a generous cook, Paulita was then in her mid-twenties, the mother of four young children. Quick-witted as well, Paulita feared the consequences of another years-long separation. "Your children need you here," she implored her husband Jacobo.

"Here" was a one-room, concrete-block house the color of tan khaki. Located in the rural, farming town of Zarajuato in Mexico's county of Calakmul, the house had an exterior latrine for a toilet, a separate lean-to for bathing, and an additional wooden structure for the raised platform where Paulita cooked the family's meals over a fire. The neighboring houses, the homes of Jacobo's parents, his siblings, and their families, sat a few yards away. Paulita lived surrounded by her in-laws.

The time was the early 2000s, and Zarajuato had no telephone service, no electricity. Paulita and Jacobo traveled two hours down a rutted road to reach the nearest full-service grocery store and the nearest supplier of cement-block construction materials. The larger county of Calakmul occupies the southernmost portion of the Yucatán peninsula, where Mexico bumps up against Guatemala and Belize. The county's tropical forests stretch into a luxuriant jade carpet. In the woods encircling

Zarajuato, migratory birds from across North America gather to cacophonous effect. Without electricity, the people in Zarajuato had no radios or televisions to mask the gruff calls of the forest-dwelling howler monkeys.

Paulita and Jacobo earned their living from the crops they farmed both for sale and for their own consumption. Money was always in short supply. Calakmul's lush countryside offered little by way of paid employment to the region's 28,000 residents.[1] This was why Jacobo's thoughts had turned to Alabama where a roofing job awaited him.

Standing next to Paulita's chubbiness, Jacobo cut a lean, wiry figure. A man of few words, Jacobo displayed a quiet intensity. Jacobo was a hard worker by nature. But as a young father of four, Jacobo had the air of a man struggling to keep up with all the responsibilities life had sent his way.

The trip to Alabama would be his second. Jacobo's first sojourn secured enough funds to pay for the cement-block house. Paulita and Jacobo's neighbors lived in houses made of hand-hewn clapboard or thatch and wooden rods collected from the surrounding forests. The cement-block structure came to 60,000 pesos, or 6,300 dollars, an astonishing sum for Calakmul at the time. Assuming full-time employment and no expenses whatsoever, it would take a typical family nearly two years to acquire the same amount.[2] Jacobo was among the very first men in Zarajuato to travel abroad, and he paid for the durable cement home in just a few short months. As an industrial roofer, he earned his money by laying flat tops on high schools, shopping malls, and big box stores across the southeastern United States.

Meanwhile, back in Zarajuato, Paulita went into construction in a different way. With her husband abroad, she purchased building materials, hired stonemasons, and supervised the house's construction. Prior to her husband's emigration, and in keeping with local custom, Paulita had rarely left the house without his permission. Now, in order to build the house, and take care of other family business in Jacobo's absence, Paulita regularly spent the day running errands.

For Paulita, the cement-block house had been the whole point of Jacobo's emigration. So when Jacobo raised the prospect for another trip abroad, she saw no need for his continued travel.

As far as Paulita was concerned, the family had met their financial goals.

Paulita also had more on her mind than her children losing their father. "The problems," as she called her arguments with Jacobo and with her mother-in-law Elvia, began from the earliest days of his travels. "The problems" were so acute, they nearly ended her marriage. Paulita feared another round of migration meant another round of "problems."

I heard about the problems first-hand while speaking with Jacobo, then in Alabama, on the telephone. I had recently returned from one of my own trips to Mexico. "Did you see Paulita?" he asked. "What was she wearing?" Jacobo had heard from Elvia that Paulita was dressing provocatively, a sign she might be dabbling in infidelity. Sensing a marital dispute I wanted to avoid, I replied blandly. Paulita looked the same as always, I said. I did not mention she had taken to new fashion in the form of tight jeans, camisoles, and make-up.

"To this day, my mother-in-law tells people that I go out with any guy that comes along, ando con cualquier," Paulita protested years later. Jacobo did end up traveling to Alabama against Paulita's wishes, and she was beginning to doubt he would return.

As Paulita told things, the problems started with rumors. Neighbors and relatives gossiped that Jacobo was flirting with a woman via one of the telephones available in the county seat. The woman lived in Zarajuato, and Jacobo supposedly invited her to join him in the United States. He even offered to advance funds for her trip. Paulita saw truth in the tongue wagging and appealed to village authorities to stop the relationship. The authorities sided with Paulita by decreeing the potential paramour should stop speaking to Jacobo on the phone and forbidding her travel abroad. While their actions did not hold the weight of law, the authorities brought formidable pressure to bear on the situation in the form of public censure.

Elvia, however, did not believe her son capable of betrayal. Seeing in Paulita's trips outside the home evidence of an affair, Elvia suspected Paulita invented the story as a diversion from her own adultery. Elvia had plenty of support for her position. Mothers-in-law across Calakmul were having similar suspicions about their daughters-in-law left alone by a son's emigration.

Although Jacobo's own sisters sided with Paulita, Elvia clung to her interpretation of events, reporting her doubts to Jacobo along with other slights, small and large, she incurred at the hands of her daughter-in-law.

It didn't take long for the family's finances to grow complicated as a result. When Jacobo felt trusting of Paulita, he sent remittances directly to her. At other moments, he sent her money but instructed her to keep only an "allowance." The remainder went to his parents to manage. When his mistrust of Paulita ran high, Jacobo only sent money to his parents from whom Paulita had to ask for her allowance. "Jacobo believes everything people say to him," Paulita lamented, and "the problems" continued.

After years of arguing, Paulita said sometimes when she spoke with Jacobo in Alabama, she felt sad for him. He talked about all the home-cooked dishes he missed. In Calakmul around the turn of the new century, black beans accompanied nearly every meal. With their strong maize flavoring, Paulita's hand-crafted tortillas made from native varieties—known as "Indian corn" in the United States—and cooked over a fire had a taste their mass-produced cousins cannot approach. Flavor is something ineffable, intangible, not so easily reproduced, yet very real. "Food means a lot more than what we put in our mouths," writes one researcher. "It is a way people communicate who they are, the group to which they belong, and who they desire to become."[3] Paulita said that Jacobo found US flavors unsatisfying.

Yet when he was in Mexico, Jacobo talked about all the US food he missed. Paulita found Jacobo's shifting food preferences puzzling. If he missed Mexico while he was in the United States, why did he insist on working in Alabama? On one occasion, their talk of food led Paulita to ask her husband, "Well, where are you going to put down roots, Jacobo? Which place are you going to choose? ¿En donde te vas a quedar?"

This book tells the stories of Mexican women whose lives changed when men in their families and communities began to travel to the United States for work. We hear from Selena, Aurora, and Rosario, women who, like Paulita, were married to emigrant men. Elvia watched two of her sons migrate and is featured in a chapter of her own. Finally, we meet Berta, a healer to whom women turned when they needed to sort out the relationship problems caused by migration.

To the best of my knowledge, none of the women has ever set foot outside Mexico. Yet together they played decisive roles in the migratory endeavor. They did so by reworking notions of marriage, gender, and sexuality in response to migration's novelties. Where much research on international migration focuses on migrants themselves (both men and women) or married couples, this book highlights the perspectives of women who did not travel, including senior women.[4] Together, their stories illuminate how gender dynamics in sending communities influence men's travels.

Why a book about Mexican women, gender, and marriage in migration at this moment in history? As I write, the net flow of Mexican migrants into the United States is at zero, meaning the same number of people entering the country is also leaving. Meanwhile, other kinds of migration have captured public attention, including the desperate moves of refugees and asylum seekers, especially women and children.[5]

My answer builds on observations that in the United States public conversations about migration have long been marked by hyperbole, misrepresentation, and propaganda.[6] This tendency is only exacerbated when government officials turn predatory toward immigrants. The messages make it difficult, if not impossible, for everyday people to identify the causes and consequences of various kinds of migration, let alone practical avenues of response.

One way to cut through the confusion is to return to principles, return to migration's foundations. What are the different kinds of migration, and how do they get their start? Whether people travel or not, their ideas about migration arise from a complex mix of knowledge, value preferences, and location within larger social structures.[7] As a result, in order to have productive conversations about migration, we need to understand the information and ideals contributing to migration from places like Calakmul. We also need an awareness of the larger context in which such information and ideals circulate.

As we learn, migration from Calakmul got its start by offering women and men the possibilities of new pleasures in life, as well as new dangers. The pleasures and dangers were inextricably bound together. The idea of interwoven pleasures and dangers draws on the work of Gloria González-López, a sociologist who examined the connection between sexuality and migration.[8] González-López depicts sexuality as a process in which people explore, seek pleasure, and enact their personal freedom of choice. Given that sexuality is enveloped in cultural norms, however, people can find in sexuality rules that restrict, repress, and create emotional hazards. In sexuality, pleasure and danger go hand-in-hand. From their gendered and generational positions, men and women have access to different pleasures. The dangers they risk are not always the same.

I apply González-López's ideas of pleasure and danger to migration more generally in order to show how, for both women and men, migration's pleasures and dangers motivated men's travels. I also show how experiences of pleasure and danger can keep migration going or put the brakes on it entirely. In Calakmul, the pleasures women found in men's absences included physical and sexual enjoyment, including new romance. Women also benefited from freedom from a life of want. They enjoyed the prospect of living a consumer lifestyle which brought with it the ability to secure a prestigious position in local society. Some women found in men's absences relief from constraining gender expectations.

The dangers women faced were equally compelling. They saw in migration the risk of emotional betrayal by intimates, a return to poverty, the revival of restrictive gender expectations, and the transformation of migrants' wives into the object of gossip and social censure. Labor migration put men at risk of alcohol dependency because, while they were in the United States, Calakmuleño men were exposed to many factors known to increase the odds of a migrant's substance abuse.[9] When men brought home with them a drinking problem, wives faced multiple hazards, including life-threatening domestic violence. All in all, divorce was a real possibility for migrant couples, as was the dissolution of other family ties.

These pleasures and dangers had roots in the way migration as a kind of globalization brought together local cultural understandings and "structural violence." Globalization is the proliferation of cross-border flows and includes the movement of people, ideas, goods, and services. Cross-border migrations in the service of integrated economies are a part of globalization, as are other kinds of travel, including tourism and study abroad. Migration in the service of global markets helps foster "transnationalism," or the establishment of communities "that cross geographic, cultural and political borders."[10]

Current thinking on globalization emphasizes that while the phenomenon promises a pervasive and unhindered flow of money, ideas, and people, on closer inspection, globalization courses along well-defined channels. Globalization simultaneously transcends and depends upon local settings.[11] As a consequence, while some aspects of globalization are visible at the local level, other aspects are invisible and beyond immediate control.

Globalization has hidden aspects that produce a "structural violence." Structural violence entails the ordinary ways people are put in harm's way as the result of large-scale social forces that perpetuate inequalities. As we see throughout the book, the dangers women associated with migration, including divorce, family disputes, and intimate partner violence, all point to the deeper workings of structural violence.[12]

What's more, as we shall see, migration's dangers and pleasures created a kind of "friction" that gave migration momentum.[13] Danger and pleasure—both the kind Calakmuleños cultivated and the kind forced upon them—motivated the migratory enterprise, propelling women and men, travelers and stayers alike into migration's global currents.

Calakmul: A New Sending Region

Calakmul may surprise US residents who view Mexico through the lens of migration. Before the year 2000, migration to the United States from this rural district of *campesinos*—people who include smallholding ranchers, timber-men, and subsistence farmers—was nearly unheard of. In Mexico, campesinos sit at the bottom of the social hierarchy. To make ends meet, they typically use temporary migration to work off-farm jobs. Yet until the turn of the new century, Calakmuleños stayed relatively close to home in their travels. Then, an expanding US economy combined with the effects of the North American Free Trade Agreement (NAFTA) to push Mexican emigration to all-time highs.[14]

NAFTA was a trade agreement implemented in 1994 that fused the United States and Mexico into a single economy by lowering barriers to trade and facilitating investment. NAFTA buffeted Mexico's countryside from many directions, and Calakmuleños counted among the millions of rural people who saw their economic options shrink as a result of the deal. Following the agreement, US farmers exported corn to Mexico at a price lower than it cost to produce. This corn "dumping" was subsidized by the US government and, for smallholding producers in Calakmul, it meant their principal harvest was no longer worth selling. Meanwhile, Mexican officials dismissed efforts to keep people on the farm. Instead, authorities sharply reduced or completely cut certain farm subsidies while gutting the markets where smallholding farmers sold their crops.[15]

These state and global efforts established a framework that influenced intimate family relations.[16] As a consequence of NAFTA and its supplementary policies, between 1991 and 2000 an estimated 20 percent of Mexico's farmers, mostly campesinos, ceased to work in agriculture.[17] The Mexican policymakers who negotiated NAFTA anticipated the agreement would displace 500,000 people from the countryside. In fact, believing that small-scale farmers held back the country's progress, they hoped NAFTA *would* push people off their farms. As a famous Mexican song intones, "*Si eres pobre te humilla la gente. Si eres rico te tratan muy bien.*" "People humiliate you if you're poor. But if you're rich, they treat you very well."[18] What Mexican policymakers did not anticipate was the exodus of 337,000 to 500,000 people from Mexico's countryside every year for fifteen years.[19] On the heels of NAFTA's passage, between 1994 and 2000 an estimated 430,000 to 770,000 people from both rural and urban areas emigrated annually to the United States (Figure 1.1).[20]

People in communities like those in Calakmul, places that had been largely untouched by international migration, were swept into its

FIGURE 1.1
A family portrait from the early 1990s, before travel to the United States from Calakmul became common. Two of the girls featured here would marry men who migrated to the United States. One of the boys became a migrant himself.
Photo: Nora Haenn

currents. By 2003, an estimated 7 percent of Calakmuleños over the age of seventeen resided north of the US-Mexico border.[21] In my experience, they all viewed their travels as temporary. It was just a matter of time before they would return home, they said. Nonetheless, their departures changed how the region's families were organized and altered the emotional landscape family members traversed to forge connections with one another.

When international migration got under way, annual household incomes in Calakmul averaged $4,000 per year, an amount that included the contributions of multiple family members.[22] In the United States, a migrant could earn that much in a single month. A handful of standout men would go on to send their families as much as $20,000 in a year. Once Calakmuleños could access these jobs, the exodus became widespread. Within a short while, even one of the few men I knew in the region who earned a steady paycheck began to muse: "Maybe I should go just to see what everyone is talking about." Some 90 percent of Calakmul's sojourners were young men in their teens, twenties, and thirties. They traveled, almost exclusively, as undocumented emigrants.[23]

With men's departures, women in Calakmul—the mothers, wives, daughters-in-law, plus one healer featured here—became participants in a kind of migration known as "men's labor migration." Men's labor migration takes place when, rather than leave for work and return home each day, men undertake jobs that require them to travel for extended periods, usually a few months to a few years.[24] In doing so, men temporarily separate from their spouses, children, and extended families. In other parts of the world, women's labor migration also takes place and has its own gendered consequences. At a global level, women are at least as likely to migrate as men, but this was not the kind of travel Calakmuleños participated in.[25]

The five women featured in this book associated with one another in what some researchers call a "migrant network."[26] They all knew each other or knew of each other, and some were kin to one another. Rosario, for example, married one of Elvia's sons (Rosario and Paulita were sisters-in-law). Rosario's brother married Selena. Aurora was once a neighbor to Rosario and Elvia. Berta's healing powers were famed throughout Calakmul. All four of the women knew at least one person who had visited Berta. When Calakmuleño men traveled to the United States, women such as Elvia, Selena, Aurora, Rosario, and Berta undertook their own odysseys in the migrant network.

Globalization, Migration, and Local Repertoires

Women's roles in making migration possible (or not) meant they were active agents in globalization. Women created and participated in the local culture that international migration, as a kind of globalization, relied upon to function. Any kind of motion, the anthropologist Anna Tsing writes, requires a certain amount of friction.[27] Globalization is no different. It requires two counterparts. In order for globalization to flow, to gain definition and shape, it must chafe against the local.

As its name suggests, men's labor migration requires a local counterpart, usually taking the form of women and other people who do not travel. Wherever it takes place, men's labor migration relies on the interdependence of both men and women, travelers and "active stayers" alike.[28]

The stories of people who stay at home tend to receive less attention, as illustrated by the difficulty posed in naming such people. While the English language has many synonyms for "migrants," we have no ready moniker for nontravelers. Yet we need such language. Active stayers retain a complex hold on the migrants in their lives, influencing where people travel, as well as whether and when migrants might return. In Calakmul, active stayers included the 93 percent of adults who remained at home yet helped shape migration more generally. In this way, the women's experiences cast light on what it means *not* to move.

Mobility and staying put are so intertwined, researchers of migration studies are increasingly using the expression "(im)mobility" to write about the connection between the two.[29] In practice, it can be impossible to separate moving from not moving. Although in popular and academic discourse migration often appears new and surprising, really the opposite is the case.[30] Both migration and stasis are part of the human condition. A key question to ask of (im)mobility is what kind of movements and what kinds of staying put are privileged? What kinds are forbidden and criminalized?

For example, the work of undocumented Calamuleño men in the United States helped create a broader prosperity that allowed some US citizens to travel legally and in privileged ways (such as to Cancún on holiday). The men's travels, categorized in US law as "illicit and subversive," contributed to the easy mobility of others "who seem to live in a borderless world of wealth and power."[31] However, neither of these kinds of travel would be possible without the immobility of women and other active stayers.

The labor put in by women was of a specific kind. In order to address the dangers and pleasures that men's travels posed, women in Calakmul had to rework their understandings of romance, marriage, gender, and sexuality. Women had to revisit their notions of gendered kin identities, sometimes defending old beliefs, sometimes deciding to live in defiance of gender norms. As we saw with Paulita's story, active stayers and migrants alike employ a "knotty set of gendered cultural considerations" when they embark on migration and later make sense of its consequences.[32] In the process, women build the family types that can bring migration to a close or transform sojourns into the multi-generational out-migration that is the hallmark of a "culture of migration."[33] This work is common to migratory settings, although often overlooked in research and popular news that focuses on migration's more tangible aspects. [34]

Elvia, Selena, Aurora, Rosario, and Berta responded to and enacted migration from within certain frameworks, drawing on particular perspectives and information. Yet as already noted, not every aspect of international migration was visible to them. In sharing the women's stories, I take inspiration from researchers who show that larger social forces and governing systems—of which globalization is one kind—can pressure families to conform to certain models. These forces are not determinative but they do define a range of possibilities and constrain people's choices. The restrictive choices are one way larger social forces enact structural violence. In the case of international migration, these forces affected how a family's men and women related to one another at the most personal levels.[35]

The strictures posed by men's labor migration have been felt across the globe for centuries. Historically speaking, the influx of Italians, Chinese, and other groups to the United States around the year 1900 was characterized by men's labor migration. (For a time US authorities forbade Chinese women to enter the country.) During the twentieth century, men from Lesotho traveled to South Africa for work, and today, Indian, Filipino, and Pakistani men go to Saudi Arabia, Kuwait, and Qatar for the same purpose.[36]

Research on this array of migratory streams shows that men's labor migration has patterned consequences.[37] Its occurrence in Calakmul, thus, had some predictable elements. In their (im)mobility, Calakmul's active stayers and travelers stumbled upon situations others have confronted over the course of centuries, although, again, these examples lie outside their understanding.

At the same time, Elvia, Selena, Aurora, Rosario, and Berta responded to migration as people with unique personalities who lived within a unique cultural setting. Altogether, Calakmul's larger migratory setting was driven by three elements: the demands posed by men's labor migration, people's personal decision making, and localized cultural norms.

The researcher Cati Coe developed the idea of a "repertoire" to help explain this process.[38] A repertoire is a toolkit, a set of cultural beliefs and practices that people employ to go about their lives. Calakmuleños drew on their repertoire to understand migration, guide their actions, and influence the behavior of others.

For example, Calakmuleños' ideas of marriage, gender, and sexuality were individual tools located within their larger repertoire. Calakmuleños recognized gender, sexuality, and family life took many forms. And in this way, their repertoire offered them a range of meanings and practices that allowed them to respond flexibly to a given situation. Repertoires are somewhat like traditions, although the word "tradition" tends to connote unchanging beliefs and practices. In contrast, repertoires are malleable, open to "revision, reshuffling, and reflection," which is why people may be able to adapt to migration's novelties when they appear.[39]

But repertoires also have their limits. Like structural violence, repertoires create frameworks of *constrained* decision making. While Calakmuleños drew on their repertoire to respond to migration, their options were finite. Some ways of thinking and acting lie outside people's repertoires altogether.

Marriage and Migration

In communities across the globe, gender is a part of people's repertoire that organizes migration. Gender influences why people want to travel (or stay at home), whether a person has any choice in migrating, and how capable people are of achieving their migratory goals.[40] In this way, migration is reflective of globalization more generally. "Producers, consumers, and bystanders of globalization are not generic bodies" but flesh- and-blood women and men.[41] Whether the globalization in question is sex tourism or clothing manufacturing (which employ mainly women), warfare or finance (which tend to be marked masculine), gender both shapes and is affected by global engagements.[42] "To view migration through a gendered lens," writes immigration expert Caroline Brettell, "means to focus on how men and women relate to one another in theory and in practice, how their experiences might differ, and how gender roles (i.e., the particular activities and tasks that are assigned to men and women) . . . might both affect and be affected by geographic mobility."[43]

Drawing on their repertoire, Elvia, Selena, Aurora, Rosario, and Berta, along with other Calakmuleños, tended to view migration's gender dynamics narrowly, through the lens of marriage. In reality, the gender changes associated with migration were broader than marriage alone. For instance, prior to migration women were nearly shut out of local political office in Calakmul, but with men's absences women acquired positions in village and county government.[44] This change did not receive much attention. Instead, people talked about marriage, and they talked about it quite a bit. As a result, throughout this book, I premise marriage as a fundamental way to understand migration.

Calakmuleños' ideas about romance, gender, and sexuality were so closely tied to their beliefs about marriage, it could be hard to separate these categories. Most Calakmuleños assumed that, apart from the rare religious vocation, heterosexual marriage was the preferred life course. Women were wives (or prospective wives) and men were husbands (or prospective husbands) within "opposite-gender" marital relationships. Although Calakmuleños recognized the existence of same-sex desire, and acknowledged gay men and lesbians within their community, nonheterosexual individuals and their families played a minimal role in Calakmuleños' assessments of migration.[45]

Instead, Calakmuleños focused on how migration changed the institution of marriage—that is, what marriage looked like before and after the advent of migration. They placed the bulk of the responsibility for holding a marriage together on wives, paying close attention to whether women conformed to ideal behavior during their husbands' absences.

Finally, they gossiped endlessly and in great detail about the messy realities couples faced once their migratory journeys were under way. People routinely said of migrant couples, "The first thing that happens is he finds another woman in the United States, and she finds another man here," sometimes adding the scientific sounding assessment that "80 percent of those marriages break up." A migrant man with no wife to return to might not see a need to return to Mexico, and people feared a wayward wife could cause her husband to remain abroad forever.

Calakmuleños were flabbergasted by migration's link to marital demise because prior to international migration, divorce was relatively uncommon in Calakmul. Calakmuleños placed a high value on marriage. Women in particular had few avenues of escape from a bad marriage. They had little access to money, and a woman's ability to leave a marriage could depend on whether she had a male relative willing to support her (and her children).

Another barrier to divorce was the belief that formerly married couples should no longer speak to each other. As rural people, Calakmuleños lived in villages, like Zarajuato, where collections of extended families clustered side-by-side. Leaving a marriage could thus mean having to move and leave behind one's relatives. All in all, Calakmuleños frowned on divorce to such an extent that once international migration became an option, some couples used men's travels to enact a separation that was otherwise socially unacceptable.[46]

Infidelity was more common, and rather than get divorced, people found excitement in affairs.[47] But like divorce, infidelity had gendered dimensions. Calakmuleños lived in a patriarchal society and subscribed to a double standard. Men's infidelities were tolerated, women's were not. Given that nearly all adult Calakmuleños were married, these men were likely fooling around with married women, but women's adultery did not receive the attention men's did. In most cases, women's adultery was shrouded in an impenetrable silence.

After international migration, Calakmul's active stayers continued to tolerate men's infidelities. Yet they viewed emigrant men's extramarital liaisons as achieving a disturbing degree of licentiousness. They looked aghast at the wives of emigrant men who appeared willing to make their affairs visible.

As we delve into migration as lived by Elvia, Selena, Aurora, Rosario, and Berta, we find these dynamics were more complicated than seem at first glance. By engaging in a new endeavor that was abetted by state authorities, Calakmuleños crossed an array of social boundaries. Migration was a "transborder" process whose effects proved highly personal.[48] Global migration pressured Calakmuleños to undergo deep-seated social change, including a reformulation of their ideas about how spouses should care for one another, a softening of the region's patriarchy, the tentative empowerment of young women, and, as a backlash to these novelties, the revival of older gender norms.

The net effect was that marital strife served as a building block of migration, at least in the short run. The patterned quality of the problems suggested Calakmuleños were correct. There was something more going on here. Infidelity and marital strain are well-documented aspects of men's labor migration.[49] And while the exact number of migration-induced divorces in Calakamul is unknown, Mexican couples involved in international migration are more likely to divorce, as are residents of communities with high amounts of outmigration.[50]

Calakmuleños were astounded at this effect on their intimate relationships because, for the most part, they could not see the abrasive counterpart that their marriages chafed against. They had little access to information about migration's globalized context or its patterned consequences. Thus, rather than understand marital strife as the friction that gave migration momentum, they understood marriage and migration as localized, personal matters.

Learning about the Personal and Invisible Sides of Globalization

In the time I have known Elvia, Selena, Aurora, Rosario, and Berta, they have spoken about migration in terms of marriage, kinship, and the many emotions intrinsic to family life. None of the women referred to NAFTA or Mexico's macroeconomic policies. The word "globalization" was not part of their vocabulary. And they seldom used the word "migration." Instead, they were more likely to use forms of the verb "to go," as in, "He went to the United States." Going implied coming back. In fact, migration-related divorce was all the more poignant because Calakmuleños said men sojourned in order to meet *family* goals.[51] In local parlance, the word "family" can be synonymous with "husband" or "wife."

Calakmuleños viewed migration as a personal matter centered on pleasure and danger because many factors influencing their experiences lie outside their purview. Globalization has a distant and invisible side in the form of policy decisions made in faraway government offices and business plans carried out by transnational corporations. The random appearance of a labor recruiter looking to fill job vacancies can also seem mysterious. But all these actions are personal for the people involved; globalization does not have an impersonal side.

Instead, the counterpoint to a personalized globalization is a concealed, out-of-reach globalization. When globalization operates out of sight, it seems to happen of its own accord. This makes globalization bewildering to the people who live it. To make sense of the changes taking place around them, people in globalized settings must turn to their repertoire from which they often develop personal explanations.[52]

In reality, the portion of globalization that operates out of view gains traction because of local repertoires and personal relationships. Observers find evidence of this friction in the recurring and patterned change globalization can create within people's intimate lives.[53] In their fears of divorce and infidelity, Calakmuleños pointed to this friction. There was something about migration per se, they said, that changed families.

In this book, I consider additional marital byproducts of migration, although Calakmuleños talked about these to a lesser extent. Many wives of emigrant men associated their husbands' travels with the men's excessive alcohol consumption and domestic violence. Domestic violence has been linked to men's labor migration because, to the extent their travels make men feel marginalized or discriminated against, they may use their patriarchal authority to exert power in the one area they still control, i.e. their families. "Powerlessness in the public sphere generates a desire to exercise more power in the domestic sphere."[54]

In Calakmul, drinking and wife battering lie within men's prerogatives, and as these tended to occur when an emigrant returned home they could be interpreted as a routine, if regrettable, reassertion of authority. Not all couples had these problems, but those who did show how migration could transform intimates. Migration might change a wife or a husband to such an extent that a person's spouse came to embody, simultaneously, globalization's personalized and mystifyingly out-of-reach qualities.

I learned these lessons by taking my own journey between globalization's invisible and personalized standpoints. I arrived to Calakmul in 1994 to carry out a year of dissertation research in anthropology, having shown up somewhat out of the blue. After spending my early twenties working with an international environmental group, I wanted to study how the creation of new environmental regulations affected the region's farmers, ranchers, and foresters. I asked my contacts at the conservation group—people who occasionally visited the region but did not actually live there—to introduce me to local residents. The local residents, in turn, connected me to places where I might conduct research.

My ties to Calakmuleños became personalized that year, as well as during subsequent visits, although between trips I was quite invisible, and Calakmuleños were not sure what exactly all the coming and going amounted to. It was difficult to explain my job as a university professor in a place that only saw its first middle school open in the mid-1990s and its first high school in the new millennium.

Nonetheless, in 1994 I got to know Elvia when I took up residence in a house next door to hers. Elvia's son Rafael, who later married Rosario, worked with me as a research assistant. In 2009–2010, I returned to Calakmul to live for a year, and it was during this period that I interviewed the women for this book. I began with Elvia and Rosario then branched out into their network to gather additional perspectives. The research included interviews with thirty people, including former and prospective migrants, as well as a variety of active stayers. I complemented these perspectives by collaborating with fellow researchers on regional household surveys [55] and, in the United States, by visiting Elvia and Rosario's male relatives in Alabama.

Throughout, I adjusted to the grief my questioning tapped in to. Previously, when I interviewed Calakmuleños on rain forest conservation, the prevailing tone of the conversations was one of anger. Campesinso were angry at a government that emitted directives with little consideration for what these meant to their working lives or their ability to feed themselves. When I asked about migration, I listened quietly to emotional, often tear-filled accounts of family fights, the loss of a loved one, and fears about what might yet come to pass.

In my personal interactions, I found that few Calakmuleños, other than political activists, had a sense of migration's distant drivers. Thus, in order to understand these social structures, I read widely on labor migration, transnational families, and gender and kinship. I also examined the literatures on Mexican history and farm policy. The historical material showed that the gap between the visible, personal side of globalization and its hidden side was long-standing in southern Mexico. As we see in the following chapter, men's international labor migration was not the first time Calakmuleños were caught up in less than transparent global structures. The gap was an enduring one and, having navigated it before, Calakmuleños had good reason to think they could do so again and keep their families intact.

In writing the women's stories, I was conscious that a book is also a globalized thing. This time, it was me inserting Elvia, Selena, Aurora, Rosario, and Berta into global connections whose reach lie beyond all our ken. As I relate their experiences, my sympathies toward their situations are sure to be clear. After all, as a researcher, I have also been a kind of migrant. At the same time, I took a few steps to assure anonymity for the women while offering an account I hope provides readers information to arrive at their own conclusions.

In addition to changing the names of the women and other people, I gave pseudonyms to villages and towns. In relating their stories, I chose aspects of the women's lives that echoed migration's effects in Calakmul more generally. Recognizing that current conversations about migration tend to narrow rather than expand understandings, I chose to leave accounts open-ended, indicate moments of ambiguity, and illustrate a range of migratory journeys. The approach aims to foster more productive conversations about migration and globalization by mimicking their open-ended qualities as Calakmuleños knew them.[56] While this book explains how globalized migration got its start, future migration from Calakmul remains an open question.

I hope readers will use Elvia, Selena, Aurora, Rosario, and Berta's experiences to explore some dilemmas we all face in today's globalized world. International migration and geographically dispersed communities are a permanent and pervasive "feature of our planet."[57] In one way or another, in our present lives or our family histories, we all partake in emigrant communities arising out of successive waves of globalization. Sometimes we are the movers. Sometimes we are, like women in Calakmul, the people who stay put yet remain connected to distant travelers.

In light of migration's personalized and hidden aspects, one dilemma that people share centers on whether and to what extent we have control over the global strands that weave us together. As we carry out our lives, are we adapting to parameters over which we have little choice? Are we unwittingly transforming our repertoires to reinforce global ties? Globalization gains traction from the friction between global and local, but it is not always clear which element carries greater sway.

People choose to participate in migration, but they are not entirely in control of either its pleasures or its dangers. This point raises the question of how we should respond to one of globalization's central paradoxes. The phenomenon can create new and welcome possibilities in our lives.

Globalization can allow for freedoms, even loves, previously unimagined. But it can also make our most intimate relationships susceptible to the actions of unknown others. Globalization can create losses from which one never recovers. Can we benefit from the liberation that globalization sometimes offers without damaging our closest connections?

Notes

1. INEGI 2015.
2. Schmook and Radel 2008.
3. Gálvez 2018: 8.
4. See review in Glick Schiller and Salazar 2013.
5. The data on the net flow of migrants comes from Passel et al. 2012. In comparison to economic migrants who travel in search of work, refugees are people who are in flight for their lives. The line between economic migrants and refugees is not hard and fast. People whose economic opportunities are so scant they feel they must move in order to survive count within both groups. At the same time, as I write, the news is filled with reports of a "refugee crisis" on the southern US border. This naming acknowledges the life-threatening situations these women, men, and children are escaping. The news relates less about what exactly these people are running from in their home countries of El Salvador, Honduras, and Guatemala. Nor does the news relate that this influx was anticipated. In addition to academic research, reports on women and children escaping violence in Central America were published by the United Nations High Commissioner on Refugees in the run up to this crisis. See Cardoletti-Carroll et al. 2015 and Goldberg 2014.
6. Chavez 2001.
7. Salazar 2011.
8. González-López 2005.
9. García 2008; Worby and Organista 2007.
10. Glick Schiller et al., 1992: ix. For an approach to globalization that emphasizes flows, see Appadurai 1996.
11. Latour 1993; Levitt and Merry 2009; Wolf 1982.
12. The definition of structural violence is from Farmer et al. 2006. See Holmes 2013 for an analysis of international migration through the lens of structural violence. See Farmer 2004 for a broader discussion of structural violence.
13. Tsing 2005.
14. See Fitting (2011) on off-farm employment. On NAFTA's role in increasing international migration, see McBride and Sergie 2017; Weisbrot et al. 2014.
15. Assies 2008; Galvéz 2018; Wise 2010.

16. Boehm 2012.
17. Zahniser and Coyle 2004.
18. The song is "El Centenario" by Los Tucanes del Norte and tells the story of a man who joins the mafia to escape poverty. Once the mafioso starts driving around in an expensive car, "*se acaban todos los desprecios.*" The scorn and contempt end. The price paid for this respect resonates with the price paid by some migrants. The mafioso travels back and forth between Mexico and the United States. He "risks his skin," living a life trapped between the Mexicans organizing his life of delinquency and the US authorities who would arrest him for his work.
19. Fox and Haight 2010; Gálvez 2018.
20. Weisbrot et al. 2014.
21. Schmook and Radel 2008.
22. Ibid.
23. Here's how Jacobo made it to the United States. While in Mexico, he struck a deal with his brother Rafael. The two farmed jalapeño chili peppers, and after selling their crops, they pooled their earnings to pay Jacobo's passage. Later Jacobo fronted Rafael the money to make his own trip to Alabama. The journeys cost thousands of dollars because, like nearly every emigrant from Calakmul, the two traveled by land, escorted by smugglers across the length of Mexico. Additional smugglers accompanied them into the United States.

Could they have traveled to the United States with a visa? If there had been a line at the US embassy in Mexico where the men could await a visa, they likely would have queued up, but for them there was no accessible legal path to entry. As manual laborers, Jacobo and Rafael might have qualified for certain visas, an H2A or H2B visa, although they had no knowledge of these. The chances they could acquire one were slim regardless. The H2A visas apply to temporary jobs in agriculture; the H2B visas to temporary jobs in construction, landscaping, and other areas. Both visas require prior connection to a US employer who sponsors the worker. The United States issues roughly 84,600 H2B visas annually. Recent data on the number of construction laborers alone indicates 1.5 million people work in that area. The United States also issues roughly 134,000 H2A visas annually. In comparison, the total number of farmworkers is an estimated 1 million, with 384,000 people categorized as "seasonal labor." (See US Department of State 2016 and US Bureau of Labor Statistics 2016).

The men faced other obstacles, too. Visa applications must be completed in English, a language they did not speak or read. The application asks for a person's home address. However, the US system of street names and house numbers did not operate in Calakmul. After the US Department of State adopted an online system, applications had to be submitted electronically. Neither Jacobo nor Rafael knows how to operate a computer.

24. Yabiku et al. 2010.
25. On women's migration, see Donato et al. 2006; Hondagneu-Sotelo 2003; Sharpe 2002.
26. Krissman 2005; Massey et al. 1993.
27. Tsing 2005: 6.
28. See Gaibazzi in Jónsson 2011: 7.
29. Salazar and Smart 2011.
30. Mahler and Pessar 2006; Piché 2013.
31. Glick Schiller and Salazar 2013: 188.
32. Broughton 2008: 569.
33. Cohen 2004.
34. Brettell 2017.
35. Boehm 2012; Hannaford 2017.
36. On Chinese labor migration, see Hsu 2000. On South Africa, see Maloka 1997.
37. Hirsch et al. 2009.
38. Coe 2013.
39. Ibid.: 16. Coe's idea of "repertoire" draws on Pierre Bourdieu's notion of habitus (Bourdieu 1992). Habitus refers to a complex whole that includes cultural ideas and skills but also the taken-for-granted ways in which people embody cultural norms. This whole constitutes a system of dispositions (i.e. outlooks and orientations), which people use to navigate their social world. The embodied aspect of habitus is relevant to a migration that centers on labor and the transformation of people's working lives. This embodied aspect of migration has received less attention but see Holmes 2013.
40. Brettell 1986; Gomberg-Muñoz 2016; Hirsch 2003; Hondagneu-Sotelo 1994; Lutz 2010; Mahler and Pessar 2006; Nawyn 2010; Pessar and Mahler 2003; Pribilsky 2007; Rodman 2006.
41. Freeman 2001: 1010.
42. Desai and Rinaldo 2016.
43. Brettell 2016: 8.
44. See Andrews 2018. In addition to men's migration creating a dearth of male office-holders, another change encouraged women's entry into politics. In 2002, Mexico passed a law requiring that women constitute no fewer than one-third of a political party's roster of candidates for office. See Baldez 2004.
45. For examples where the nonheterosexual orientation of a migrant or family member did matter see Cantú 2009; Carrillo 2017. In Mexico, where

support for diverse sexual identities is uneven, advocates prefer the acronym LGBTTTI, which stands for lesbian, gay, bisexual, transsexual, transgender, transvestite, and intersexual. Discrimination on the basis of sexual orientation is barred by federal law in Mexico, and nearly two-thirds of respondents in one survey reported supporting gay marriage (Kohut 2014). As of writing, same sex marriage is legal in about one-third of Mexico's states. Yet the other two-thirds are under considerable pressure from a vocal opposition not to legalize gay marriage. In the United States, the Transgender Law Center at Cornell University and OutRight International are two organizations that report on LGBTTTI matters in Mexico. In Mexico, El Clóset de Sor Juana is one of a variety of groups advocating for LGBTTI rights.

46. Migration as an acceptable way to end a marriage is not uncommon. As the anthropologist of the Philippines Jim Eder pointed out to me, migration in that country is known as "the Filipino divorce."
47. Hirsch et al. 2009.
48. Boehm 2012; Faier 2011; Stephen 2007.
49. Hirsch et al., 2009; Maloka 1997.
50. Frank and Wildsmith 2005.
51. See also Adler 2015; Hondagneu-Sotelo1994.
52. James 2005; Moran-Taylor 2008.
53. Adelman 2017; Boehm 2012; Menjívar 2011.
54. Brettell 2017: 89.
55. Radel et al. 2017; Schmook et al. 2018.
56. See the approach advocated in Pielke 2007.
57. Stephen, 2007: 34. See also Tsuda et al. 2014.

CHAPTER 2

A Very Brief History of Globalized Calakmul

On the archaeological site of Calakmul: "Calakmul is a modern name, according to Cyrus L. Lundell, who named the site. In Maya, ca means 'two', lak means 'adjacent,' and mul signifies any artificial mound or pyramid, so Calakmul is the 'City of the Two Adjacent Pyramids' . . . [The archaeological site] was first reported by Cyrus Lundell in 1931. A year later he informed [famed US archaeologist] Sylvanus Morley of the site's existence and the presence of more than 60 stelae. Morley visited the ruins himself on behalf of the Carnegie Institution of Washington in 1932."—(https://en.wikipedia.org/wiki/Calakmul, accessed July 16, 2018)

"What is it about trekking through the jungle that sends ominously [sic] cool vibrations sprinting down my spinal column? It's wild, unpredictable, mysterious—kind of like walking into a strip club in Vegas on your 21st birthday—it's just an exhilarating (and intimidating) place to be. So when I heard about this massive ancient Mayan site embedded in the remotest of remote jungles near the southern end of Mexico's Yucatán Peninsula, I couldn't resist the opportunity to make the trip down to check out the remains of what was once among the most influential sites in the history of the Mayan Empire: Calakmul." —Damian James, travel blogger and photographer (https://gringowithagreenbag.com/tag/calakmul/, accessed July 17, 2018)

On the internet, Calakmul's most recent global engagements are hyped as thrilling adventures. The English-language World Wide Web describes the archaeological site and surrounding biosphere reserve—which both share the name "Calakmul"—in tales of exotic travel. At 1,787,000 acres, the Calakmul Biosphere Reserve is three times the size of the Great Smoky Mountains National Park and larger than the Grand Canyon National Park. Although the ancient city, also called Calakmul, once sat at the heart of a densely populated countryside, for various reasons, Native peoples abandoned urban life in the area around 800 CE. Most moved elsewhere on the Yucatán peninsula, leaving forests and wildlife to repopulate the stone monuments and farms left behind (Figure 2.1).[1]

This history gives some travelers the impression that Calakmul is a blank slate. The region seems to be a place where visitors can free themselves from the weight of their own personal history.

But the word "Calakmul" also applies to the county encompassing the reserve, and here a sense of emptiness is difficult to sustain. This

FIGURE 2.1
The ancient ruins of Calakmul, surrounded by the Calakmul Biosphere Reserve. Both the ruins and the Reserve connect the larger county of Calakmul to global travelers. However, most county residents have never seen the site. Transportation is expensive in Calakmul, and for many this sort of local tourism is an unaffordable luxury.
Photo by PashiX. This file is licensed under the Creative Commons Attribution-Share Alike 4.0 International.

larger region of 28,000 people is undeniably a multi-dimensional global crossroads. (The Spanish-language internet includes far more coverage of the county than its English-language counterpart.) Both now and in the past, global inroads have run through the county of Calakmul, gaining momentum from the area's distinctive features.

To capture this density of global engagements, I find it helpful to contemplate two types of global interaction. One type centers on the place itself. Calakmul is home to exceptional natural resources. And ever since the late 1800s, international groups of one kind or another have coveted its flora and fauna. The American archaeologist Cyrus Lundell, who gave the Calakmul archaeological site its name, came across the ruined city while working for a US chewing gum company. Chewing gum was originally manufactured from the sap of a tree located only in Calakmul and the neighboring tropics.[2] Later, Calakmul and its assets were packaged for consumption by hardwood and lumber concerns, environmental groups, heritage preservationists, tourists, and tour operators, as well as academic researchers like me.

In this chapter, I summarize the region's history as a provider of environmental services by using my own collection of regional souvenirs. The souvenirs illustrate global ties, which are eminently tangible. Objects that evoke Calakmul's globalized history can be purchased, shared, and displayed.

Calakmul's global engagements also center on the people who live there.[3] This additional type of interaction is difficult to memorialize in objects because it is rooted in migration of another sort. During the second half of the twentieth century, poor farmers from throughout Mexico moved to Calakmul. They followed paths first laid down by chewing gum and lumber companies, transforming temporary camps into permanent settlements. Campesinos cleared land for crops and cattle ranching. They changed the region's character by fashioning an agricultural landscape.

Calakmul's agricultural pioneers are now an older generation of women and men in their sixties, seventies, or eighties. These parents and grandparents to younger generations born in the region multiplied the global strands running through Calakmul by bringing with them their own histories of globalization. Those encounters took place elsewhere in Mexico and, like Calakmul's own globalized past, reached back generations. Some family genealogies are entangled with intersecting and reinforcing global ties such that, for them, globalization came to form a sticky, inescapable web. In this chapter, Elvia's family exemplifies this aspect of Calakmul and how globalization can become personally embodied in people.

Many researchers argue that past globalizations gave rise to today's international sojourns, although it can sometimes be difficult to connect the dots.[4] Did these histories lay the groundwork for men's labor migration?

I am persuaded that historical antecedents did establish a basis for men to travel from Calakmul to the United States. Some historical events—although not all—created conditions in Calakmul that left families with few economic opportunities. Other global ties fostered within the local cultural repertoire an understanding that migration was common and could be used to address personal and social problems. Altogether, localized mobility combined with job scarcity, the shrinking economic options resulting from NAFTA, and other state policies to establish a foundation for men's international sojourns.[5]

Souvenirs from Calakmul

Souvenirs provide easy entrée into any region's history. Souvenirs, like other objects, can hold within them "the residue of some moment or person that is 'set apart' from the everyday."[6] Gifts, for example, remind us of the giver. Souvenirs recall treasured moments and faraway places. Tourism promoters regularly offer travelers collections of souvenirs that reflect a region's uniqueness. These objects are meant to be invested with meaning and used as containers of experiences, emotions, and relationships. Souvenirs often seem trifling to one person but invaluable to another who sees in them symbols of a rich history.

Over the years, I have built up a collection of memorabilia from Calakmul that symbolize my time in the region. I have also sought out objects that conjure experiences and relationships beyond my life there. These objects recall the past, but they tend to be of recent origin. Until the advent of international migration, Calakmul's history of globalization left little by way of enduring material wealth.

A Jigsaw Puzzle

One of my favorite souvenirs is a children's jigsaw puzzle, a replication of an ancient jade Mayan mask. Sold by Mexico's National Institute of Archaeology and History to tourists, the puzzle is a playful introduction to pre-Columbian history. Native people living in Calakmul one thousand years ago left a profusion of archaeological sites scattered across the county.

For me, Mayan-themed trinkets remind me of Calakmul's history of encounters between Indigenous people and foreigners. This history began with the arrival of Spaniards in the 1500s and continued during Spain's colonization of Mexico during the sixteenth, seventeenth, and eighteenth centuries. Throughout this time, Spaniards required that Native people under their domain undergo forced labor. Calakmul, however, lie just outside the empire's grip. The region was too far from centers of power and too densely forested to control effectively. Some Spaniards did try to marshal military conquests into the region; the idea was to acquire trade routes, then controlled by Indigenous people. A few military excursions into the region did take place. However, for the most part, during Mexico's colonial period Calakmul acted as a "refuge region" for Indigenous people.[7] By fleeing to Calakmul and forming a handful of forest communities, Indigenous people gained political independence.

For these Native peoples, the term "Maya" as it is typically used today would have been unintelligible. "Maya," as a description for an ethnic group, was first used by Spanish colonialists. The invention gained wider application when nineteenth century archaeologists used it as a label for Indigenous groups across southern Mexico, Guatemala, and Honduras.[8]

Today, people in Calakmul rarely use the term. Archaeological ruins, they say, were built by *los antiguos* or the ancient ones. The ethnic groups of interest to Calakmuleños are people who repopulated the area during the twentieth century, a mix of Indigenous and non-Indigenous people. Calakmuleños use the word *Mayero* to describe speakers of Yucatec Maya, people who migrated to the region from elsewhere on the peninsula. Berta, who we meet in chapter 7, is *Mayera*. Calakmul's largest Indigenous group speaks *Ch'ol*. Ch'ol is related to Yucatec Maya in the way French and Spanish are branches of the same language family. Ch'ol speakers arrived to Calakmul from Mexico's state of Chiapas. Elvia (chapter 3) and Rosario (chapter 6) both speak Ch'ol. Finally, non-Indigenous people act as an "unmarked category" in Calakmul, a group that has no specific name, although Calakmuleños call people from Veracruz and Tabasco, the Mexican states most heavily represented in the non-Indigenous population, *Veracruzano* and *Tabasqueño*.

Non-Indigenous people serve as a counterpoint against which Indigenous people are defined and typically stand above Indigenous people in Mexico's social hierarchies. Selena (chapter 4) and Aurora (chapter 5) are non-Indigenous women. Their examples show how prejudice against Native people in Mexico is significant, even extending into families of mixed ethnicity. The social contempt coerces Indigenous people into abandoning their Native identity and is part of a larger tendency toward "colorism" in Mexico. Colorism takes place when people of darker skin color, regardless of their ethnicity, rank below people of lighter tones. In Mexico, dark skin color is associated with campesinos (who work outside in the sun) and Indigenous campesinos in particular.

All this makes for a complicated identity setting in Calakmul, where non-Indigenous people may ignore or hide their association with Indigenous heritage. Selena's family, for example, does not believe themselves to have Indigenous ancestors. Selena married a Ch'ol man, but a casual visitor to her household would only see the family's non-Indigenous character. Aurora's family, in contrast, recognizes some Mayero heritage, but they do not claim this identity for themselves. For both families, distancing themselves from an Indigenous identity also distances them from societal bigotry.

Which is to say, despite its use in tourism and archaeology, Calakmuleños rarely claim a "Maya" identity. Instead, "Maya" as a blanket term tends to be used by visitors to Calakmul in a way that obscures ethnic variety both in the present and in the past.[9] For me, the children's jigsaw puzzle among my souvenirs encapsulates how history and identity are often reformulated and simplified by those in power in order to facilitate global exchanges.[10] Simple messages regarding Calakmul's "Mayan" archaeology belie the region's very complicated ethnic landscape in the past and in the present.

A Photograph

Like many travelers, I usually have a camera at the ready. As a result, my larger stock of memorabilia contains lots of photographs. The collection includes one image that depicts a man who seems to defy gravity. He hugs the upper reaches of a tree trunk, with four feet of air floating between him and the ground. The photo recalls Calakmul's history as a producer of *chicle*, the sap of the *chicozapote* tree that formed the essential ingredient in chewing gum.[11] Until the invention of a synthetic version of the tree's sap in the 1940s, Calakmul was one of the few places manufacturers could secure the gum. A closer look at my photograph shows that the gum tapper ascends the tree via metal spikes tied to his shoes. A rope wrapped around his waist and the tree trunk prevents him from falling backward.

Chewing gum became incredibly popular in the United States after US companies that had acquired extensive landholdings in Calakmul convinced the US Department of Defense to incorporate the candy into soldiers' rations. This was around the time of the First World War, and manufacturers claimed chewing gum would ease soldiers' stress. The resulting boom in gum production lasted through the Great Depression, with as much as 95 percent of Mexico's chicle harvest destined for US markets.[12]

North of the border, chicle was incredibly profitable. In ten short years, between 1919 and 1929, one chewing gum enterprise, the Wrigley family (makers of Juicy Fruit and other varieties) used its revenues to create a sprawling empire. The company built the Wrigley Building on Chicago's Miracle Mile, purchased Santa Catalina island off the coast of southern California, and bought the Chicago Cubs baseball team. The Cubs' ballpark became known as Wrigley Field.[13]

The image in my photo album calls to mind the source of this wealth, the men and women who worked Calakmul's forests. The man climbing the tree carries a machete on his belt. He used its sharp edge to cut v-shaped grooves into the tree bark. The grooves carried the tree sap down the tree trunk and into a basin on the ground, where the sap began its own journey to the United States.

A Wooden Serving Set

In addition to its archaeology and chicle production, Calakmul is known for its timber. A set of carved, wooden serving utensils among my souvenirs, a gift from a Canadian biologist who studies Calakmul's wildlife, evokes this history. As with chewing gum, US business interests helped shape the timber industry. Investors, such as the Pennsylvania-Campeche Land and Lumber Company, first secured rights to cut Calakmul's forests in the late 1800s.[14] As the twentieth century got under way, the region's physical isolation made it impossible to transport heavy timber to distant markets. And some of these companies later went into chewing gum production. Calakmul's apex as an exporter of tropical cedar and mahogany would arrive in the 1950s and 1960s when motorized transport became available.

At this point, Mexican-owned enterprises took a leading role in the industry. During the mid-century, Mexican authorities restricted foreign access to the country's economic resources, especially land. The aim here was to assure Mexico's wealth benefitted Mexicans as much as possible. For example, despite the profits made from chewing gum, the industry left little in Calakmul apart from seasonal camps, a network of mule trails, and a single airplane landing strip. In twenty-five years of visiting Calakmul, I only once encountered a durable building that served as an office for a chicle outfit. The building had been abandoned to cattle that roamed an adjoining pasture.

Mexican-owned timber interests took a different approach by investing in permanent infrastructure in Calakmul. One company built a town—self-consciously modeled after company towns in the United States—complete with a primary school, hospital, church, a baseball team, and shotgun style houses for workers. The company widened the old mule trails to accommodate logging trucks and shipped lumber from the single landing strip. In the early 1970s, the company bulldozed a path to the nearest city and made way for a paved road. For the first time, Calakmul's forests became easily accessible by car.

US concerns still played a crucial role in Calakmul's timber economy. The United States was the principal market for Calakmul's lumber, which traveled through Cuba to Florida. Prior to construction of that paved road, US manufacturers facilitated transport to market by making payments in airplane diesel. US manufacturers went so far as to take up residence in Calakmul to ensure sawmill production met their specifications.[15]

By the 1980s, the environmental effects of the timber exports could be felt throughout the region. Calakmul's forests were largely depleted of valuable wood, after which the larger forestry companies ceased working in the region. Stepping in to take their place, Mexican and international environmentalists, along with US archaeologists, began to pressure for a protected area that would safeguard the archaeological treasures and thinned-out forests. In 1989, the Calakmul Biosphere Reserve came to fruition. Its ancient city, still mostly buried under the tree canopy, was designated a World Heritage Site by the United Nations just a few years later. Today, both the city and the reserve are World Heritage Sites, and the protected area endures as Mexico's largest for tropical ecosystems.

The carved, wooden serving utensils in my collection were made by Calakmul artisans for a tourist market attracted to the reserve's ruins and wildlife. Given by one university researcher to another, both of whom were originally drawn to the region's ecological profile, the wooden fork and spoon reflect connections between science and tourism that often go unnoticed.[16]

My collection of souvenirs reminds me that twenty-first century tourists, researchers, and other foreign visitors to Calakmul are just the latest in a stream of international sojourners. We follow in the footsteps of Spanish colonial authorities, US chewing gum manufacturers, US archaeologists, US timber companies, and other international actors.[17] When I admire the jade mask puzzle sitting on my office shelf, peruse a file of photographs, or serve dinner guests with the wooden fork and spoon, globalized Calakmul briefly comes alive. The region's history of global connections, condensed and symbolized in object form, pop up to create a distinctive moment in my everyday life.

Globalization in Person

When I arrived to Calakmul in the early 1990s, people were quick to describe the region as a "Wild West," an agricultural frontier run by men willing to use force and intimidation to get their way. Calakmul was not a particularly appealing place to live. What I didn't know was that many Calakmuleños had tried very hard *not* to move there. The typical campesino who settled the frontier first attempted to make a living elsewhere. Families had moved an average of 1.5 times before arriving to the region. Many relocated with their extended families, collections of brothers and sisters who moved together as adults after forming families of their own.[18]

Why did so many Calakmuleños feel they had no choice but to live in the region? By exploring people's family histories, I learned that long before international migration came along, Calakmuleños had been exposed to other kinds of structural violence, often as the result of globalization. This structural violence could demand both mobility and confinement of different kinds.

Elvia is the oldest woman we meet in the following pages. Her personal and family history thus offers the widest period in which to explore how globalization shaped people's (im)mobility. As an Indigenous woman whose family has lived in the Americas since time immemorial, Elvia's history and that of her ancestors provide a window onto the way globalization's effects upon families can last for generations.

To begin with, from the time Spanish colonial authorities governed Mexico and into the 1930s, Indigenous men in her home state of Chiapas were forced by the state to undergo temporary labor migration. Women remained home. The men built roads and other public works; they were also assigned to private businesses. The work ethic and physical stamina men developed in their farm fields allowed them to grow the crops that fed their families, but it could also be put to use by elites eager for cheap labor.[19] State authorities argued the men's labor was required in lieu of taxes. At the time, Chiapas had very little by way of a market economy where people could secure money to pay their taxes in cash. Thus, state authorities demanded men work. "Migration is Chiapas's oldest story," writes the historian John Womack, noting laborers could work away from home for three to six months of the year.[20]

In the late 1800s, a new kind of forced labor became prevalent in Chiapas, when German nationals colluded with Chiapas's non-Indigenous officials to secure Indigenous labor. The Germans were backed by US investors.[21] At the time, Elvia's great-great grandparents and other Ch'ol people lived on ancestral lands. They supplied their own needs by farming a mix of crops which included cacao beans for trade. Unknown to them, stockholders in the United States had formed enterprises with an eye toward the region's cacao groves. Cacao and coffee require similar ecological conditions, and the US market for coffee was booming as the result of yet another strand of globalization. The mass arrival of Europeans and Asians to the United States was driving an economic expansion. Luxury goods, such as coffee, were becoming affordable to a growing group of the newly moneyed.[22]

Businesses such as the "Pennsylvania Plantation Company" and the "German American Coffee Company" responded with plans to convert Chiapas's family farms and independent villages into mega-sized agribusiness landholdings. Headquartered in Omaha, Nebraska, where its principal investor was a US Congressmen, the "German-American Coffee Company" hired German nationals to run the "El Triunfo" estate. El Triunfo would ultimately acquire 43,000 acres of Ch'ol land and field a workforce of 3,000 (Figures 2.2a, 2.2b).[23]

Ch'ol leaders protested the loss. In 1891, one assembly of leaders wrote authorities to complain that a group of men had invaded their lands. The men were ripping out cacao plants and putting in coffee. But Ch'ol efforts to protect themselves never had much of a chance. Chiapan authorities were busy selling land throughout the state and pocketing

Triunfo Coffee 40¢ per lb.
in 1 and 2 lb. sealed cans.
Trinidad 35¢ per lb.
in 1 lb. sealed cartons.
G. A. Blend $1.00 per can
in 3 lb. sealed cans.
La Cruzada 30¢ per lb.
in 1 lb. cartons.
Iowa Brand 25¢ per lb.
in 1 lb. cartons.
Tumbala 20¢ per lb.
in 1 lb. cartons.
Quezal 50¢ per can
(after-dinner Coffee) in ½ lb. sealed cans.

These Coffees are grown on El
Triunfo Plantation in the Sierra
Madre Mountains, 4,000 feet
above sea level, and are absolutely
pure and undoctored.

*Use one teaspoonful of Quezal Coffee
to each after-dinner cup.*

The German-American
Coffee Company.

General office, 406 Greenwich St.,
New York City.
Chicago office, 100 Washington St.
Des Moines office, 300 Observatory Bldg.

FIGURES **2.2a and 2.2b**
An advertisement for the German-American Coffee Company. Calakmuleños participated in many kinds of globalization before migrating internationally. Calakmuleños who originated from Mexico's state of Chiapas recalled their ancestors farmed coffee in slave-like conditions circa 1900. Germans managers, backed by US investors, oversaw the estates. The ties to the United States were invisible to workers whose descendants mainly associate the era with Germany.
Credit: Charles Bender

the profits. Within two decades of the letter's writing, independent Indigenous communities with secure control over their property had all but disappeared in the state.[24]

Foreign investors bought land that was already occupied, and then charged rent to Ch'ol and other Indigenous Chiapans. By demanding rent in the form of labor, German plantation managers acquired the workforce they needed to run the new estates.

Elvia's grandparents lived and worked on the very first estate established in Chiapas, the Finca Morelia. The family planted, weeded, and harvested the Finca's coffee trees. They sorted and dried coffee beans in preparation for their shipment to the United States. During this time, Native people could still be pressed into migrant labor, but they were otherwise confined in virtual slavery to the estates. Among other tactics, plantation managers maintained private jails and discouraged construction of roads in Ch'ol territory that might connect Indigenous people with the outside world.[25]

During the era of the large estates, power often manifested in both mobility and immobility. Across the globe, wherever "coffee production depended on large plantations, the owners relied on slavery or forced labor."[26] Chiapas's plantations were no different. Indigenous people were largely bound to the plantations and, otherwise, required to move according to managers' demands.

The idea that there was power in choosing whether to move or stay put was not lost on Ch'ol people. An elderly man recorded by the anthropologist José Alejos García in the early 1990s offered this history of coffee: "The *patrón* is sitting there, healthy in his comfortable seat . . . watching everything. He doesn't move. After all he's the *patrón,* isn't he? The poor people are the ones suffering from work."[27] One escape from abusive overseers entailed fleeing to another estate. The demand for labor was high enough that some Indigenous people could secure a limited autonomy by moving and playing estate managers off one another.

When Elvia was born in the 1940s, Mexico's federal authorities were in the process of breaking up the large coffee estates. As it had with timber in Calakmul, Mexico's federal government pulled its support from foreign ownership of coffee estates in the mid-century. The profits from coffee were also ending up mainly in the hands of foreign investors, and authorities sought to keep more of that money in the country. Nonetheless, the social relations surrounding coffee production reverberated throughout Elvia's life. The break-up of the estates was a violent endeavor that took decades. Although US and German investors largely left Chiapas in the 1930s, the Mexican growers and buyers who replaced them used every trick they could think of to maintain dominance.[28]

By the 1950s, the coffee estates around Elvia's home village were still large enough to cause land shortages. Thus, when Elvia married during the 1950s, she and her husband undertook their very first migration to secure farmland of their own. They moved about 75 miles away to a village where family and neighbors, young couples such as themselves, were setting up a new community.

Elvia lived in this home for seventeen years, after which she and her family left because, "There were often murders in that town. People drank and then they fought." The violence came close to home when one of Elvia's brothers-in-law became its victim. In the first half of the twentieth century, the murder rate in Ch'ol communities neared eight times that of any modern US city. In the wake of the plantations' violence, aggression seeped into Chiapas's social life and interacted with other political currents to propel ongoing social unrest for decades.[29]

Escaping the violence, Elvia, her husband, and their children fled to yet another frontier agricultural community, a place where people from their extended family awaited them as neighbors. This part of Chiapas was tropical and did not have the growing conditions that coffee required. Nonetheless, in her new home, Elvia encountered a new confluence of global structures which, in the 1990s, combusted into a conflagration.

Globally Induced Migrations

When I met Elvia in 1994, she had just arrived to Calakmul with a group of 150 people, all in flight from a civil war. Popularly known as the Zapatista Uprising, the war was fueled by a buildup of "kindling." The Chiapas where Elvia grew up was a society with large gaps between the wealthy and the poor and a disregard for the rule of law (especially by government authorities). In the 1980s, multiple advocacy groups became active in Chiapas, each uncompromising on their own particular vision for Mexico's future.

With the right sort of friction, kindling erupts into flames.[30] The friction that helped inflame the Zapatista Uprising included new kinds of globalization such as financial investments made by the World Bank and the US Agency for International Development. Chiapas's long-standing ties to global coffee markets had a role to play as well. For Elvia, this convergence turned her into a refugee. During the 1990s, she and her family underwent three relocations. At the end of these moves, Elvia was living in Zarajuato in a house made of thatch and wooden rods collected from the surrounding woods. Her sons stood poised to emigrate to the United States.

Globally Induced Migration in Chiapas

The Zapatista Uprising earned its name from the *Ejército Zapatista de Liberación Nacional* (EZLN) or Zapatista Army for National Liberation.

In the years leading up to their rebellion, the EZLN organized Chiapas's Indigenous people to fight persistent discrimination. As one of Elvia's fellow refugees explained to me, this is what Zapatista organizing looked like on the ground. In the late 1980s "a woman began arriving to the village, a woman named Hermila. We nicknamed her Mila. Mila used to teach school, she brought games to the village and was working with the women on a sewing project. Everything was going along just fine."

The EZLN was especially concerned that Indigenous campesinos were losing access to their livelihoods. International investments in cattle ranching—paid for, in part, by the World Bank and the US Agency for International Development—had squeezed out smallholding farmers in some parts of Chiapas. In other parts, Indigenous people became desperate for a safety net when coffee, by then the principal cash crop for thousands of campesino families, saw a 50 percent drop in price on the global markets. In the late 1980s, members of the International Coffee Organization, which sets production quotas to guarantee the world's coffee farmers a minimum price, failed to come to an agreement. The resulting drop in the global price of coffee meant families in Chiapas's coffee growing regions saw their incomes shrink by 70 percent.[31]

For the EZLN and their supporters, rather than protect campesinos from globalization, Mexico's government was committed to deepening global ties. And even more threatening than sinking coffee prices or investments in cattle, for the EZLN, NAFTA presented the biggest global menace. Just before NAFTA's creation, US investments reportedly controlled two-thirds of the Mexican economy.[32] NAFTA promised to expand this control. The EZLN was alarmed that to make way for foreign investment in land, Mexico's federal authorities had changed the country's constitution and removed protections for smallholding farmers, such as Elvia.[33]

Before NAFTA, Mexico's constitution promised campesinos that state authorities would help them access land. Furthermore, Mexico's agrarian law made it difficult to sell the land campesinos farmed. These measures shielded smallholding families from the predatory land merchants who were common throughout Mexican history. The Zapatistas took their name from Emiliano Zapata, an early twentieth century opponent of the haciendas and plantations that, like the coffee plantations, were notorious for booting campesinos off property that rightfully belonged to them. Zapata helped write the portion of Mexico's constitution guaranteeing campesinos access to an agrarian livelihood.

The EZLN was so concerned that NAFTA would drive Indigenous people off their land and into deeper poverty that they chose January 1, 1994 as the day to launch their uprising: the same day NAFTA was set to go into effect. Elvia's neighbors—who listened as Mila's sewing classes turned into political meetings—believed the EZLN offered a new beginning.

Elvia, her family, and friends disagreed. They argued campesinos should negotiate with the government, not fight it with weapons. For their opposition to the war, Elvia and others were coerced into fleeing. In the uprising's early and most tenuous days, the Zapatistas "tolerated no dissent or pacifism: the minorities had to leave."[34] And at first, the war's refugees included mainly people unaffiliated with the Zapatistas.

As state forces rallied, the tables turned. The Zapatistas and anyone viewed as opposing the state came under pressure to switch allegiance, face persecution, or move on. At the war's end, between 50,000 and 84,000 people were displaced. An estimated 99 percent of the exiled were Indigenous, although Native people make up only 17 percent of Chiapas's population.[35]

Globally Induced Migration in Calakmul

Fleeing Chiapas to Calakmul, Elvia and family first landed in the village of Orozco. This is how Orozco's elected village leader, himself Ch'ol, explained why he accepted the refugees into his community: "They came fleeing the guerillas. *Vinieron jodidos en plano,* they were completely screwed. They didn't have anywhere to stay."

But the refugees' arrival worried other villagers. Before Elvia moved to Orozco, the village was home to a hundred fifty people with 6,400 acres of land. There was certainly room to spare, but half the village's residents were non-Indigenous, Spanish-speaking campesinos. Fearing their new status as an ethnic minority, these non-Indigenous campesinos pressured the refugees to move on.

Elvia and her relatives wanted to live somewhere they could trust their neighbors. They chose the Calakmul Biosphere Reserve as their second landing spot in the region. An abandoned village inside the protected area promised safe harbor. The site was isolated enough the group would not have to worry about nearby communities. And since everyone living in the village was a friend or relative, the group did not fear treachery.

Elvia and her family, nonetheless, faced daunting poverty. The refugees had been forced to leave most of their belongings in Chiapas when they fled the war. Their few, short years in Orozco was not enough time to build a farming base. Inside the biosphere reserve, the refugees started their farm operations, again, from scratch. So perhaps it isn't surprising that while living inside the reserve, Elvia's sons began to plot their trips to the United States.

Before the men could head North, however, the family had one more move to make. Under government orders, they packed their belongings, hired trucks to carry their things over unpaved roads to chisel a town and cropland out of dense rain forests. Elvia and other people living inside the protected area were relocated from the reserve to Zarajuato.

Across the world, the number of protected areas and the territory they encompassed tripled during the 1980s and 1990s. Mexico proved to be one of the world's most avid creators of these ecological monuments. Mexico also followed international trends in viewing humans as fundamentally destructive toward forest ecologies.[36] This meant creating protected areas that were empty of people, a philosophy that underpinned the forced relocation of Elvia and her family (Figure 2.3).[37]

FIGURE 2.3
The village of Zarajuato soon after Elvia and her family were relocated there. Residents had to clear forests to build houses, so tree stumps and other debris have yet to be removed. Notice the houses are constructed of materials gathered from the woods. The two houses visible here belonged to related families. Close living allowed for an easy flow of information and gossip.
Photo: Nora Haenn

Globalization's Invisible History

"Calakmul is an ancient Mayan city located deep within the jungle in Campeche state near the border with Guatemala. Not many people make it out this way due to it's [sic] remote location.

Surrounded by the Calakmul Biosphere Reserve, it's extremely remote, and a true adventure for those looking to get off the beaten tourist trail in the Yucatan Peninsula. You're likely to see only a handful of other visitors."

—Matthew Karsten, travel blogger
(https://expertvagabond.com/yucatan-peninsula/, accessed July 16, 2018)

It's easy to understand why tourists see Calakmul as isolated from the rest of the world. The language of "discovery" is common in travel writing, which encourages readers to imagine they are the first to stumble upon hidden treasures.[38] In this sense, tourism is not that different from men's labor migration. Both kinds of mobility are rooted in "imaginaries, from the most spectacular fantasies to the most mundane reveries."[39] In Calakmul, the biosphere reserve's expansive forests translate into a tabula rasa upon which international visitors can project the desires that led them to board an airplane in the first place.

Globalization's invisibility adds to this effect. The Wrigley building, after all, is in Chicago. Lumber sold in the United States disappeared into the larger market for wood products. Ch'ol and other Indigenous people from Chiapas have a rich lore surrounding German coffee plantation managers. But they do not talk about US involvement in coffee production because the US investors were entirely hidden from them. This meant that when Elvia's sons migrated to the United States, they did not know the dollars they chased were the same currency that enslaved their ancestors.

Globalization's opaque quality persisted throughout the twentieth century and into the present. The regulations surrounding NAFTA were written in dense lawyer-ese and are now housed on computer servers. Pricing decisions made by the International Coffee Organization were beyond the influence of Chiapas's coffee growers. And monies invested by the World Bank and the United States Agency for International Development traveled from one bank account to another, again, in ways beyond local sway. Both the Zapatista uprising and the influx of Chiapan refugees to Calakmul can seem, at first glance, to be entirely regional events. But they were also the by-products of global encounters.

What Calakmuleños could see of globalization was the family ties that protected them against its abrasiveness. Family members served as one other's safety net. Families worked together and stuck together through globalization-induced migrations. Whether they arrived to Calakmul to work in gum tapping, timber, or as frontier farmers, Calakmuleños said they moved to the region accompanied by family or to be with family already living there. Family made it possible to move along; family made it possible to stay put; family gave Calakmuleños the flexibility in mobility that they needed in the face of globalization's structural violence.

Notes

1. Folan Higgins et al. 2015; Mann 2006.
2. Schwartz 1990.
3. By describing global engagements as place-based and people-centered, I echo Bruno Latour's use of the railroad as a metaphor for globalization. Like railroads, global paths have definition and shape. Global paths are constructed by real people with specific destinations and timetables in mind. Calakmul's natural resources have served as global infrastructure, in the same way stations and tracks provide infrastructure for train travel. During the 1970s and 1980s, logging in Calakmul even focused on the production of actual railroad ties.

   When people ride trains, they bring to their journeys personalities, histories, and experiences of their own. Passengers use their repertoires to create meaning from their journeys. Yet passengers cannot move about as they please. They must ride the tracks available to them. And although Latour does not mention this aspect of rail travel, anyone who has been on a train knows they offer different kinds of accommodations. A single line of railroad cars may include first-class and second-class offerings. Some passengers—like the Central American migrants who cross Mexico atop a train so awful it's popularly known as "The Beast," see Martínez 2014—hitch rides on boxcars designed to carry freight.

   For Latour, because globalization is always rooted in specific places and specific people, the global is "local at all points" (Latour 1993: 117).

4. Just some of these include Hsu 2000; Mahler and Pessar 2006; Piché 2013; Pribilisky 2007; Wolf 1982.
5. Cohen 2004; Gálvez 2018; McKeown 2010; Thornton 1998.
6. Newell 2014: 188. See also Mauss 2002.
7. On trade routes and military incursions see León Pinelo 1958; Dumond 1997; Jones 1989. On refuge regions, see Aguirre Beltrán 1967.
8. Restall 2004.
9. Magnoni et al. 2007.
10. Wolf 1982.
11. Mathews 2009.
12. Ponce Jiménez 1990.
13. Matthews 2009.
14. Hart 2002.
15. Haenn 2005. Calakmul's timber era had yet another global tie. The Mexican business that built a company town did so by recruiting a group of Polish refugees from World War II. As the town's original social core, these families provided an instant set of services as bakers, cobblers, and carpenters, see Vidal Angles et al. 2005.
16. West 2008.
17. The US archaeologist William Folan pioneered much of the work at Calakmul in the 1970s and 1980s. He was one of the first advocates of a protected area to safeguard the ruins.
18. Haenn 2005.
19. This sort of labor subsidy is common in international migration as well. See Gaibazzi 2013.
20. Womack 1999: 5; cf. Rus 2003.
21. Winters 2014.
22. Jiménez 1995.
23. Alejos García 1999; Benjamin 1989.
24. Alejos García 1999; Rus 2003. How did authorities sell other people's land? The answer offers a lesson in the power of distant actors. During the colonial period, the land on which Chiapas's Indigenous people lived was technically owned by the Spanish king. This "crown land" meant the Spanish state was a landlord to Indigenous people and was one reason the state could require forced labor.

Mexico's independence from Spain nullified the crown's ownership. Mexico's new authorities sponsored land surveys to catalogue who owned what land. But surveyors drew maps "of private properties without actually measuring them" (Holden 1994: 67). All someone had to do was announce that he or she owned a piece of land. Surveyors characterized crown land as "untitled." Separately, Chiapas's authorities ruled non-Indigenous people could lay claim to "untitled" land (Rus 1983).

The people most familiar with changing property laws and the know-how to influence land surveys tended to already work in government. As a result, the people who acquired titles to Indigenous land were mainly federal employees, state governors, and their family members. These non-Indigenous elite, in turn, sold the titles, and by extension Indigenous people's labor, to foreign coffee enterprises.

25. Bobrow-Strain 2007.
26. Tucker 2011: 39.
27. Alejos García 1994: 55; see also Toledo Tello 2002.
28. Reyes Ramos 1992.
29. On murder rates, see Alejos García 1994:115. On the legacy of violence, see Womack 1999. Examining municipal archives in Palenque, Chiapas for the years 1924 to 1934, Alejos García calculates a murder rate of 3 for each 1,000 inhabitants which can be standardized to 300 murders per 100,000 residents. In comparison, according to the Chicago Tribune newspaper, murder rates in that city during the 20th and 21st centuries ranged between 8 and 35 per 100,000 residents. See https://www.chicagotribune.com/news/breaking/ct-history-of-chicago-homicides-htmlstory.html, accessed June 22, 2019.
30. This history of the Zapatista uprising relies on Collier 2005 and Womack 1999. While the Zapatista Uprising provided the most dramatic example of flight from rural violence, Calakmuleños who migrated to the region from elsewhere in Mexico also described fleeing social unrest and violence carried out with impunity (see Haenn 2005). Research on the larger problem of impunity in Mexico is extensive. The non-profit WOLA reports on such impunity and advocates for change: wola.org.
31. Harvey 1998: 177–178.
32. Fernández-Kelly and Massey 2007: 103.
33. The Zapatistas did not anticipate NAFTA's effects on emigration. In the aftermath of the agreement, Chiapan communities that lie outside international migration streams also became swept into their currents.
34. Womack 1999: 43.
35. At the time, Mexico gave no official recognition to these internal refugees. The figures are from Arana Cedeño and del Riego 2012; see also Pérez Vázquez et al. 2013.

36. Brockington and Igoe 2006; Naughton-Treves et al. 2005; Haenn et al. 2014 and Haenn 2016 describe how conservation in Calakmul and elsewhere has failed to imagine a campesino-based environmental protection.

37. This philosophy did not always predominate in Calakmul. In the early 1990s, a reserve director sought to cultivate campesino support for the reserve. Having watched elites in Mexico grab valuable land time and again, he aimed to encircle the protected area not with fences but with local people who had an interest in the reserve's survival. See Haenn 2005.

38. Pratt 1992.

39. Salazar 2011: 1.

CHAPTER 3

Elvia: Marriage before Migration

In the late 1990s, Elvia Dorado listened as her twenty-year-old son, Rafael, told her about his plans to travel to the United States. As an Indigenous woman, Elvia's ethnic background was noticeable in her appearance. She was born in the 1940s, and like most Ch'ol women of her generation she wore skirts and dresses but never trousers. Her face was clean of makeup. Traditionally Ch'ol women never cut their hair, and Elvia wore hers parted in the middle and tied at the nape of the neck in a low ponytail. The hairstyle accentuated her round face and her sky-high cheekbones.

Elvia had two ways of understanding Rafael's pending emigration. One way was the temporary labor migration that Elvia knew well. Indigenous people like the Dorados have a centuries-long history of men's temporary labor migration. For as long as they could remember, the Dorado men made ends meet, as did other campesinos, by traveling for work. The Dorados planted corn, beans, and squash for themselves alongside whatever crop fetched a price in the market. But this work rarely provided them enough. Men traveled off-farm to work in pairs or groups, alongside friends and family who could keep one another company and offer each other protection. Sitting at the bottom of Mexico's social hierarchy, the Dorados and other Indigenous people regularly faced the discrimination that comes with being part of a marginalized minority. Their work-related travel reflected this fact.

In some ways, Elvia's family was built to withstand the hardships of men's travel for work. By the late 1990s, however, another kind of travel had threatened to separate her from her children, and it was these more recent events that led her to hear Rafael's announcement with alarm.

In the decade before Rafael's decision, Elvia had tenaciously held her family together through two moves. First, they fled the Zapatista Uprising. Then, after the Calakmul villagers who originally welcomed the Dorados balked at the family's permanent residence in their community, Elvia shepherded her six children (some grown and with families of their own) to an abandoned village site inside the Calakmul Biosphere Reserve. When Elvia learned of Rafael's plans, the family was facing its third move in ten years, after state authorities told them they must leave the biosphere reserve.

The involuntary moves had left Elvia concerned she might not be able to keep her family together. Fearing Rafael's loss to emigration, Elvia made a pronouncement of her own. Turning to the surest way she knew to bind her son to home, she told Rafael it was time he married.

At twenty, Rafael was an aging bachelor in Calakmul terms, and Elvia figured a good wife would tie him to Mexico. Even if he traveled abroad, she believed he would have to return to his family at some point. To be clear, Elvia was not making a suggestion; she was giving an ultimatum. If Rafael refused to marry, Elvia said, she would no longer cook for him or wash his clothes.

The pronouncement placed Rafael in an unbearable position. Among his fellow campesinos, cooking and cleaning were women's work. As a man, Rafael would break strong social taboos if he dared undertake either task. While the distinction between men's and women's work often placed Calakmuleña women at a disadvantage, Elvia knew there were some situations where the difference could also give women power.

For years, the otherwise mild-mannered Rafael fumed at his mother's interference. "She said this was some kind of tradition handed down by the ancestors," he would mutter resentfully. For Elvia, marriage forever firmly bound men and women to both their spouses and their larger extended families. Marriage, she decided, would keep Rafael close to home.

W hen Elvia Dorado turned to marriage to prevent her son's emigration, little did she know that international migration would change the very institution she thought kept her family united. This chapter explains marriage as Elvia's generation understood it, a model that prevailed in southern Mexico throughout the twentieth century. The model endured the strains of her family's multiple relocations in the run-up to international migration. As we learn, Elvia's son Jacobo married Paulita in the traditional way five years before his trip to the United States.

Elvia sought to force Rafael into a similar kind of marriage because, for her, marriage was an indissoluble bond, essential to transforming youths into adults. Marriage was *how* young people grew up and took on adult responsibilities. Elvia did not want Rafael to migrate, but if he did, his marriage would assure his travels were akin to those of his brother's, those of an upstanding, mature individual who sojourned in order to care for family, not run away from it. The durable nature of marriage meant, for Elvia, that Rafael would have family he felt obligated to return to. He would not succumb to the pleasures or dangers that awaited him abroad.

Neither Elvia nor her sons or neighbors anticipated that marriage as they knew it would serve as the principal point of friction that could spur continued international migration. Marriage could buffer a young man against migration's perils and encourage his return. But it could also be the reason he stayed away permanently.

Unmarried at Elvia's House

Elvia's insistence on marriage as essential to a life properly lived reflected her society. Elvia's neighbors and family gossiped about Rafael's bachelor status. They wondered what was taking him so long to settle down and joked that his prospective wife was probably called *Soledad*, a common woman's name in Mexico that means "loneliness." Elvia could not have been immune to the wagging tongues. In other ways, however, she ran a household that was different from many in

Calakmul, a household where she set the course, regardless of what others had to say.

In accordance with local gender norms, most Calakmul families gave the impression that the senior man was the family's authority, but this was not the case with the Dorados. Elvia and her husband, Raimundo, had been married for four decades, but Elvia rarely followed his lead. Raimundo was a sweet, fun-loving, but unreliable man with a drinking problem. He once famously lost 20,000 pesos—almost eighteen months' worth of earnings—to a swindler at a bar. At her house, Elvia was the more influential partner, and from this position she could force Rafael to marry.

Elvia's strength of character was on display from the very start of our friendship. When we first met, I had just arrived to the village of Orozco to embark on a yearlong stay. Elvia and her family had arrived in the same village from Chiapas a few months earlier. The Dorados were my next-door neighbors, and I often dropped by to chat with Elvia after first being announced by the scrappy, knee-high, yellow dog that barked uncontrollably to alert the family to anyone's approach.

To reach the Dorados' one-room home, I walked a narrow footpath cut through secondary forests. The path led from my house downhill to a clearing Raimundo, Rafael, and Jacobo had carved by machete out of a stand of taller woods. In the clearing, the family had planted corn and other basic crops. They had also speedily erected a house. The one-room structure stood fifteen feet long by ten feet wide, with a sloping roof that reached seven feet at its tallest. The building materials were cheap and readily harvested from surrounding forests. The roof was a thatch of dried grass. The house's walls were made of vertical poles cut from saplings and tied together with vines.

As I crossed the home's threshold, made of the same sturdy rod that girded the walls, I stepped onto a dirt floor. Immediately, I found myself maneuvering around the basic necessities of life the family had packed into the small space. With family members coming and going, the house could be occupied by as many as nine people plus an infant or two. Clothes were draped over thin, plastic ropes tied to the rafters. To my left sat a raised bed for sleeping. The family had lashed together additional poles to create the bed and then covered the whole thing with a blanket and clothing to cushion its bumpy edges. On the wall above the bed, two hammocks were wound into knots for storage. Unloosed and stretched across the center of the room, the hammocks served as extra beds. To the right of the entrance and leaning against the wall were cardboard boxes the family had flattened out. Laid out on the ground, these served as a third sleeping space. The family's kitchen sat in the building's far-right corner. There, Elvia had laid down a three-stone hearth and Raimundo had tied a long plank to the adjacent wall to act as the kitchen counter. Catty-corner to the counter, the family had somehow squeezed in a water barrel and a bench wide enough to accommodate three people.

From my perch on the bench, Elvia offered me lessons in Ch'ol cultural beliefs. I learned that Elvia thought of herself as a Christian and took it as a matter of course that the Bible was the word of God. But through her localized faith, she viewed the Bible and church teachings as compatible with ideas of faith healing. Elvia's grandmother and older brother had both been healers. And Elvia herself occasionally worked as a mid-wife, but only when an auspicious dream—such as a visit from the prospective newborn—inspired her to do so.

Elvia also taught me how important matrimony was to her. Her lesson came mainly in the form of frank disbelief at my own unmarried status. At the time, I was twenty-six years old, and an astounded Elvia wondered how it was possible I had arrived at such a late stage in life without a husband. She peppered me with questions:

"And you're not married?" Elvia asked.
"Have you never been married?"

No, I responded.

"And you have no children? Not even one?"
"You live alone? You're not afraid to live alone?"

The questioning managed to make me feel inadequate, a frame of mind I came to experience again and again, as Elvia reviewed my answers with one daughter and then another who, in their own amazement, wanted to hear my answers for themselves.

"Really, you're not married?"
"And you have no children?"
"You're not afraid to live alone?"

Seeing how surprised they were, I did not venture to tell the fuller story. I wasn't sure how I could explain the cultural gap between us.

Growing up in the United States, I was encouraged to strike out on my own before finding a mate and settling into married life. Like many of my peers, I spent my twenties working or going to school while either living alone or sharing a rental with other unmarried women and men of my age group. I lived in communities safe enough that young people could get along without family protection. I figured I would fall in love and marry at some point, probably to a man I met through family, work, or school. My husband and I would set off on a life in which we supported each other's aspirations. Our shared quest for personal fulfillment would include deciding for ourselves where we would live. Until then, as long as I had the income to do so, I was relatively free to travel and explore new places.[1]

If I had given this fuller account, I doubt it would have made things any clearer to Elvia. Her idea of wedded life was quite different from mine. For both of us, marriage expanded the social connections and resources people needed to get by in life. For both of us, marriage was a foundation of family life. But our ideas of *family* also differed in many ways.

For Elvia, the fact that I lived *alone* was as astonishing as the fact that I was single. From Elvia's experience, women almost never lived without some kind of family protection. Thinking back to Elvia's concerns for my safety, I should have asked more about these worries. (Later in our friendship, she actually sent one of her children to my house to keep me company.) Had she never known a place where it was safe to live alone?

More generally, Elvia found it unimaginable that a person could live without extended kin surrounding her, family who participated in her daily existence, from sun up to sun down. It would not be going too far to say her understanding of human life is that it should be lived as part of a group—that each individual is a node in a web of relationships such that no person should live without kin nearby. Marriage brought together individuals to expand this web of relationships across families and into future generations.

Getting Married at Elvia's House

Not long after meeting Elvia, I had the chance to see in practice how she thought young people should go about finding a life partner. The occasion was the marriage of her son Jacobo. The Dorados' life as refugees had left them scrambling to build a farm, but the younger Dorados had found that their new home also created tantalizing possibilities for romance. In 1990s Calakmul, villagers typically looked to their neighbors as potential mates. At the time, the region had few paved roads and scarcely a public bus that might allow young people to travel outside their villages. With little opportunity to make new acquaintances, the young people of Orozco saw the appearance of refugees as a boon.

Jacobo had his eye on Paulita, but to meet, the youngsters had to work around a number of social taboos. In Calakmul, marriageable men and women were not supposed to speak to each other. Their elders believed that any male-female relationship outside marriage had the potential to become a romantic connection. Sexual longing, people said, could bubble up from beneath the surface of the most casual interaction. The briefest chat could lead to sexual relations. Since sex before marriage was forbidden, it was best if unmarried men and women avoided these interactions altogether. Public dating was unheard of and would only become an option in Calakmul's larger towns in the new century.

The burden of managing such delicate matters was decidedly gendered. Proscriptions against speaking with the opposite sex or engaging in premarital sex weighed more heavily on women. According to patriarchal norms, men were assigned the role of initiating romantic relations; women were expected to demonstrate their honor by keeping men in line.[2] Going further, women were supposed to refrain from behavior that gave men an opening to act. Calakmuleños cautioned chaste young women to remain as home bound as possible and not to leave the house without their parents' permission. (Once married, a woman would need her husband's permission.) Young women were warned they faced danger in solitary sojourns, usually from predatory men. When a woman did run errands or take some unavoidable trip, she was expected to keep a reliable witness on hand at all times who could later corroborate her whereabouts.

How then were Jacobo and Paulita supposed to connect in a way that would lead to marriage? The way Elvia saw things, given village life, it was easy for young men and women to observe each other from afar. So ideally a young man would notice a young woman and let his parents know he was interested in her. Then the prospective groom's parents would visit the young woman's parents to make an offer of marriage. Preferably, a young woman's parents would consult with her to see whether she was amenable to the match. This had been the case for Rafael's siblings, none of whom underwent an arranged marriage.

Nonetheless, during my years in Calakmul, I heard of enough cases in which parents accepted or rejected a suitor's request without their daughter's input to know that Elvia was right. Some parents did choose their children's marriage partner, although usually the person with the least say in the matter was the bride rather than the groom. Historically, parents in Mexico chose their children's spouses because people believed family interests were more important than individual preferences.[3]

As a result, young people who wanted to choose their marriage partners carried out their courtships in secret. Jacobo and Paulita worked around the prohibition against speaking to one another by taking advantage of tiny Orozco's two observable sources of entertainment.

Every day in the late afternoons, after finishing the day's farm chores, Orozco's teenage men gathered to play soccer. As the sun went down, the youngsters returned home for a bath, and then gravitated to the one house in town that owned a television. These were the days before satellite and cable television became widely available. With eligible men walking after dark between the soccer field, home, and the television, any young woman who slipped out of her house was likely to put her herself on the path to romance. Although Orozco parents publicly claimed to keep careful watch over their daughters, many turned a blind eye to their daughters' evening wanderings.

Jacobo and Paulita exchanged whispered words in the shadows that lie just beyond the glow of Orozco's street lamps. Jacobo then initiated an engagement by asking his father and mother to accompany him to visit Paulita's parents. Raimundo made the marriage request to Paulita's parents on Jacobo's behalf.

Paulita's parents confirmed with their daughter that she was supportive of the marriage, and once there was agreement on all sides, the families joined in a few additional, ritual visits. Elvia and Raimundo brought Paulita's parents gifts of the kind farm families appreciated, including chickens to add to the family's flock. A bridegroom and his parents might bring offerings of liquor to a prospective bride and her parents or, if the family abstained from alcohol, soft drinks.

Following custom, the wedding ceremony was an act of little fanfare. Paulita simply moved in with Jacobo, Elvia, Raimundo, and the rest of the Dorados. Families with the resources to do so might precede the move with a festive meal, but Elvia and Raimundo were too poor at the time to afford this, as was Paulita's family. Most Calakmul families were of similar means, so Jacobo and Paulita's marriage began in a way that was conventional at the time.

Prior to the advent of international migration, these ritual steps were enough to create binding marriages.[4] Once married, it was difficult for a couple to separate, especially as both partners' parents had pledged to support the union. A young husband might turn his back on his wife, but this was considered especially scandalous as he had initiated the relationship. Family and neighbors gossiped that such a young man's parents should discipline him to behave appropriately. People recognized that a newlywed wife, in a moment of remorse, might try to return to her parents. If she had no children—no extra mouths to feed—and extremely kind parents, there was an outside chance she would be accepted. Parents were more likely to admonish a doubting daughter to return to her husband. A woman who abandoned her marriage was considered socially disgraced.

When Paulita and Jacobo wed, the Dorados were still crowded into that one-room, thatched house. In order to accommodate Paulita's arrival, Jacobo and Raimundo went about remodeling. One day, I stopped by to find the men had opened up a wall and fashioned a small alcove that the couple could use as their marital bed. Father and son had built the addition with poles gathered from the surrounding forest and the same reddish grass that served as roofing material for the rest of the house. The alcove offered a private niche for the newlyweds, but it was also an extension of the family's shared quarters. The alcove sat adjacent to the cooking hearth and, on later visits when I took my usual perch on the bench, I chatted with Paulita while she and Elvia shared the family cooking.

Elvia's idea of a proper marriage entailed a beginning period during which newlyweds lived with the husband's parents while the couple learned how to be husband and wife to each other. Anthropologists describe this residential system as "patrilocal." When international migration became an option in Calakmul and marriage served as its local counterpart, it was the practices and ideals associated with patrilocal residence, including the system's inherent tensions, that gave men's travels momentum.

Women in Patrilocal Residence

As a general outline, patrilocal residence requires that newlyweds spend the first years of their married life with the husband's family. Young couples do so because, as was the case with Jacobo and Paulita, they have few resources of their own to set up a household. After a few years, a young couple acquires what they need to build a house of their own.

They usually do so somewhere close to the man's family. Because of this, patrilocal residence shapes men's and women's lives in different ways, with most of its benefits going to men. By creating families built around a male line, the residential system reinforces men's authority in the home and in society at large.

In Calakmul, young people did not always follow this formula to the letter. Within any society, young people's post-marital living arrangements can vary considerably, as the choice of where to live depends on a range of factors. Yet even when young Calakmuleños did not strictly adhere to the tradition, its details offered a framework from which families made marital and, later, migratory decisions. When Calakmuleños said they migrated to meet "family" goals, family could mean the larger, patrilocal household that was crucial to young people's ability to secure the resources they needed to get by in life.

Recalling her father's advice on the eve of her own marriage and entry into patrilocal residence, Elvia remembered that he counseled she had better pull her weight: "Now that you're married, you're going to know what work is. If you sit down, where will your next meal come from?" Patrilocal residence is typical of smallholding farmers, whose heavy workload requires the large, extended families the system fosters.[5] The advice Elvia received from her father highlighted this aspect of the married life that awaited her. For farm families like Elvia's, marriage was a way of socializing the younger generation into assuming full responsibility for their part of the shared workload. As a woman living with her husband's family, Elvia would be evaluated on how hard she worked while relying on Raimundo's family for food, clothing, and other necessities.

Because the senior couple in a patrilocal household supervises the labor of the younger couple, when a bride entered the home of her husband's family, she essentially went to work for her mother-in-law. During Elvia's youth in Chiapas and later in Calakmul, gender ideals positioned men as having ultimate authority in the household. Mothers, however, attended to young people's day-to-day education. This meant a mother-in-law monitored her daughter-in-law's diligence, the refining of the young woman's housekeeping skills, as well as her other behavior.

In Calakmul, brides entering patrilocal residence were often already trained in the duties expected of them. When it came to dividing up chores, most Calakmul families followed a gendered division of labor in which women and men carried out complementary tasks.

Men built houses, cultivated crops, or sought out temporary jobs off the farm. Men's work tended to take place outdoors and away from the family's residence. Women animated the house by overseeing the many activities that took place there: caring for children, hand-washing laundry, raising chickens and turkeys, and preparing tortillas and meals from scratch. Children participated in this division of labor, with boys and girls often beginning to take on their respective chores around the age of eight or nine years old.[6]

Despite this early training, relations between a mother-in-law and a daughter-in-law were often fraught. For the older woman, given the patriarchal world in which she lived, her authority over a daughter-in-law was one of the few arenas where her authority consistently superseded a man's. Some women in the senior generation used this power abusively, a pattern common to patrilocal settings throughout the world. Daughters-in-law living with their mothers-in-law can be "expected to be obedient, submissive, and stoic in the face of gratuitous mistreatment, both psychological and physical."[7]

Intense mistreatment could rise to the level of family violence. Domestic violence takes place in all societies and tends to be heightened when other forms of violence emanate from the larger society.[8] In Calakmul, the larger society followed patriarchal ideals that functioned, in part, by allowing men's aggression toward women and senior women's aggression toward younger women. While not all Calakmuleños agreed with these premises—including Elvia—family violence was habitual enough that its presence was taken for granted and impinged on relations between mothers-in-law and daughters-in-law.

Elvia did not describe her own stay in patrilocal residence as particularly difficult. Still, under the system's associated norms, she waited years to acquire social status. As a young wife, Elvia earned some respect when she began to have children. She gained additional status when she gave birth to sons, who would carry on the male line. She acquired greater prestige still when Jacobo brought Paulita into the family. "Elvia has a daughter-in-law in the house," people said to indicate this special period. A woman who was a mother-in-law was no longer expected to be submissive and self-effacing. As a mother-in-law, a woman came into her own as a "strong, experienced, and practical" adult.[9]

Elvia and Paulita's time together also appears to have gone smoothly, but if there had been problems, Elvia's new social standing would have given her the upper hand. Young men were hesitant to contradict their mothers, and a young wife in conflict with her mother-in-law often found her husband unwilling to back his bride. On the contrary, a son entrusted his wife to his mother, just as Jacobo entrusted Paulita to Elvia. A young wife in disagreement with her mother-in-law might find the older woman coercing her son to take her side against his wife. Some mothers-in-law went so far as to push their sons to discipline young wives through the man's own violence.

Escape from Patrilocal Residence

Given these stressors, in the early twenty-first century, when migration and other social changes gave young Calakmuleños the chance to speed their way to independence, many sought to do so. Living with a man's parents brought "problems," they reported to me a bit cryptically, and it was better for the marriage if a couple could live "apart," as a nuclear family. Young couples were cryptic because they did not want to insult the older generation upon whom newlyweds were still dependent. Quietly, they turned to migration as a way to *change* family.[10]

Although they bore the brunt of the strain of patrilocal residence, young women were not the only ones pushing for change. One aspect of patrilocal residence often escaped attention because young men were hesitant to raise their concerns publicly. To complain in the open would be tantamount to doubting their families and the prerogatives men enjoyed as a result of their family position. Some young men in Calakmul resisted the presumption that they would forever live with or next door to their parents. They found the arrangement suffocating, and they wanted a way out.

Which is to say that both young men and young women growing up in Calakmul looked to marriage as a way to enter adulthood, but their paths were not exactly the same. Young women looked to marriage as the way to leave their parents' home. But marriage did not give young men the same escape. If men wanted to seek out pleasures beyond the family or a reprieve from family life, including married life, they traveled to work.

In 2015, I visited Elvia in Zarajuato, the place where she was able to create a permanent home. More than fifteen years had passed since she arranged Rafael's marriage. With her son's thoughts turned to the United States, Elvia knew Rafael was not thinking about finding a partner. So when Elvia told her son it was time he married, she also informed him she had chosen his bride.

Rosario was the quintessential girl next door, someone Rafael had known for as long as he could remember. With her terra cotta skin and tawny-streaked hair, Rosario is often described as blonde by other Mexicans. At most, she stands five feet tall. In my mind, I frequently have to reconcile Rosario's diminutive frame with the spark of energy she exudes. Her dynamism has the effect of adding inches to her stature. Before marrying, Rosario was "una persona muy alegre," an infectiously happy person. I would run into her in the company of her parents and siblings, from whom she stood out with her ready laugh. Like most seventeen-year-old women of her generation, Rosario rarely left her home unaccompanied and had little notion of life outside her family.

Elvia chose Rosario because she was of marriageable age and her bright personality was well known. For Elvia, it also mattered that Rosario's vivaciousness was complemented by an impressive work ethic. Elvia viewed marriage as a social contract in which happiness arose for men and women when they worked for each other. From Ch'ol perspectives, "A hardworking man will lack for nothing . . . A hardworking man . . . is worthy of a hardworking woman."[11]

After they wed, however, Rafael and Rosario engaged in years of relentless arguing. Rafael thought of this girl next door as something close to a sister, and he resisted married life. Rosario had been hesitant about the marriage, but she understood what was expected of her and did not object strongly to her father's suggestion. Her resentments appeared after the wedding.

Neither of them anticipated that in many arranged marriages, love appears slowly, cautiously. After more than a decade of unease, that is how Rafael and Rosario's marriage evolved. On that trip to Zarajuato, I stayed with the couple and found a respectful and caring partnership the two had worked hard to achieve.

During my visit, Rafael agreed to accompany me to his mother's house. As we walked to Elvia's, I joked that we should brace ourselves. As seemed inevitable in any conversation with Elvia, we were about to be on the receiving end of some strong opinions. Her constant refrain: "My children never visit me. Neither do my grandchildren."

*Elvia's children would always be too far away for her satis-
faction, although it was hard to imagine how they could live any
closer. Six of Elvia's nine children lived a three-minute walk from
her home. With her sons abroad, Elvia came down with a case of
"colic," a common intestinal illness that struck her, she claimed,
because "it's not good when they leave." Her children close at hand
still pitched in when a crisis arose. Nearing seventy years old,
Elvia broke her hip and was confined to a blue plastic armchair
that doubled as her walker. Elvia's daughters took turns helping
her cook, clean, and bathe. The family reviewed the doctor's diagnosis at length, questioning whether it was accurate and whether
it had been wise to decline a hip replacement surgery. With their
trust in traditional medicine, everyone doubted the hospital's doctors were reliable.*

*The afternoon Rafael and I visited, Elvia sat in her kitchen,
her armchair tucked between the raised platform of her cooking
fire and a table that kept pots, plates, and other essentials within
arm's reach. The house has no running water, so Elvia asked Raimundo, then enjoying a late-life sobriety, to run outside and refill
a bucket.*

*I was beginning to think of the two as an elderly couple in
their twilight years when Elvia brought me up short. "Why didn't
you visit sooner?" she asked. Here it was Thursday, and she knew
I had been in town since Tuesday. Elvia barely let Raimundo get
a word in when she asked about Jacobo, who was then in Alabama. Had I spoken with him? Was it true he had injured his
hand on the job?*

*While Rafael did eventually migrate to the United States
and marriage did bring him back to Mexico, Jacobo's story was
another matter. The cumulative strain of separation eventually
ended Jacobo and Paulita's marriage.*

*I told Elvia I had not spoken recently with Jacobo, but later
learned it was true a mishap at work had required surgery on his
hand. Jacobo is a roofer, a job that ranks among the most dangerous occupations in the United States.[12] During three months
of recovery, Jacobo could neither bathe nor dress himself without
help. His new, bilingual partner, Wendy, proved indispensable to
his recovery. When his employer declined to offer worker's compensation and demanded Jacobo be back on the job, Wendy used*

her knowledge of US labor law to intervene. Send Jacobo home and pay worker's comp, she told the company, or she would call immigration authorities herself: "If you want to play hardball, we can do that." Jacobo required so much care after the accident, he had little choice but to move in with Wendy. While living together, the couple began to think of themselves as married.

Elvia knew none of these details. She still viewed Paulita as Jacobo's wife, despite the couple's estrangement. Elvia's idea of marriage included the notion that married couples stayed together forever, no matter what. Thus, Jacobo had not yet broached the topic of his new partner with his mother.

Because I had yet to learn the details myself, I had no news to offer. So Elvia turned our conversation to the other topic foremost in her mind, food. During the decade when Elvia was forced to undertake three moves, she feared for her ability to feed her family. Back in the 1990s, in addition to questioning my marital status, Elvia announced to me with her typical frankness: "When you visit, I want to offer you something to eat. But I don't always have food to offer." Elvia and Raimundo had been able to stay put in Zarajuato long enough to rebuild their farm. The newfound food security brought out Elvia's inner gourmand. She was keenly interested in whether her next meal would be a good one, and my negligence in alerting her to my arrival meant a missed culinary opportunity. "Why didn't you send word of when you would visit?" she asked. Guests are always a good excuse to prepare a nice chicken soup, and Elvia was in the mood to eat.

Notes

1. This description, of course, is particular to my upbringing. In the United States, there are a number of models of courtship and life-long partnership, of which marriage is just one kind. Readers interested in pursuing this topic may consider Finkel (2017), Stack (1983), Weston (1991), and the larger body of work by Gerstel and Sarkisian, especially their book on *Nuclear Families Values, Extended Family Lives* (2012).

2. Placing the responsibility on women for managing opposite-sex relationships lays the groundwork for men's coercive behavior. When women are not allowed to say "yes," men can interpret "no" to mean "maybe" or "not yet" and press the matter accordingly. I thank Mary

Wyer for pointing this out. For more on the question of consent in sexual relationships, see Beres (2007).

3. Esteinou 2005, 2007; Stross 1974.

4. The shared secret of their courtship and the shared conspiracy of breaking norms also helps tie a couple together. Twenty-five years after her marriage, the secret continued to hold sway over Paulita. When we reviewed her courtship, Paulita blushed and became charmingly awkward. She still hesitated to admit her and Jacobo's pre-marital rendezvous.

5. Netting 1993; Pasternak and Ember 1997.

6. See also Wilk 1991.

7. Brown in Pauli 2008: 174.

8. Adelman 2017; Menjívar 2011.

9. McClusky 2001: 169.

10. See also Pauli 2008.

11. Pérez Chacón 1993: 245.

12. According to the US Bureau of Labor Statistics, roofing is the fourth most dangerous job in the United States after (in descending order) logging, fishing, and piloting/engineering an aircraft, see Johnson 2017.

....

CHAPTER 4

Selena: The Model Wife

Selena's mother waved me into the family's kitchen, where I found the twenty-six-year-old hunched over a notebook, a cell phone pressed to her ear. She was speaking with her husband, Lázaro, who was working as a roofer in Alabama. At the time, Lázaro was four years into his trip, having left six months after the couple's daughter was born.

Lázaro came from a Ch'ol family, but Selena did not. And while she loved her husband, she was less enthusiastic about his Indigenous identity. Viewing patrilocal life with Indigenous in-laws as a step down, Selena opted to spend Lázaro's absence with her parents in a town far from his family. Until Lázaro's return, Selena's mother was her principal guardian.

Joining Selena in the kitchen, I had the feeling I was intruding on a private moment. Selena spoke with Lázaro in hushed tones, apparently about the household accounting written in the notebook. She appeared to be reviewing house-building costs and taking direction on how to proceed. Selena regularly phoned Lázaro to ask about finances and seek other guidance. Migration from Calakmul began in the years before internet and cell phone service became widely available. But Selena lived in one of the first Calakmul towns to get cell service, so the couple could speak frequently and confidentially. In comparison, rural places like Zarajuato (where Elvia lived) had no cell service and just one public telephone. The public phones were usually located in a shopkeeper's home, where they were sure to channel any conversation directly into local gossip networks.[1]

A frequent topic of conversation between Selena and Lázaro entailed her seeking permission from him to leave her home for anything other than a necessary errand. She asked Lázaro if she could attend a dance, to which the answer was no. She asked if she might join the Parent Teacher Association at their daughter's school, to which the answer was yes. And she asked if she might try expanding the family's income by selling cosmetics door-to-door. Lázaro was lukewarm to the idea, but he did not oppose the job. Selena was teasing when she asked about the dance, as dances were notorious sites of drinking and flirtation. Selena carefully kept to innocent activities. She rarely left the house without a family member who could readily confirm her whereabouts should anyone later question where she had gone.

Four years into Lázaro's emigration, however, Selena was growing tired of keeping up appearances. The couple's principal goal for the migratory trip was to build a house. Things were not going as planned, and, now, it was unclear when Lázaro might return. Selena desperately missed her husband, and the phone calls were not enough to make up for his absence.

Selena and I moved from the kitchen to a living area, where her mother joined us to review the couple's migratory endeavor. Like the rest of the clapboard home, the living area was meticulously clean. It was also crammed to capacity: a full-sized bed, a double-door mirrored wardrobe, a stuffed chair, and a love seat. The love seat faced an entertainment console with a television, a DVD player, a stereo, and decorative items. Sitting side by side on the bed, Selena and her mother bore a striking resemblance to each other. Both had long, narrow faces. Both had shoulder-length, wavy black hair and dark skin that hinted at African ancestry.

The furniture and electronics surrounding us were de rigueur in well-appointed migrant homes, but the items belonged to Selena's parents, who received money from their three sons living in Atlanta. The only object on display belonging to Selena was another popular purchase, an oversized, framed photograph. Selena's picture had a migratory twist. She had asked the photographer to make it appear as if Selena, Lázaro, and their daughter, Lydia, had posed together, which he was able to do using computer software. The photograph was Selena's only image of her small family.

A playful, four-year-old Lydia ran into the room. Pointing to me, Selena gave the girl a lesson in manners: "Say hello to our guest. She knows your father. You do not know your father, but you will." Selena maintained a stream of conversation with Lydia about Lázaro, building up a father's image for a girl who had no memory of him. "Lydia has a mountain of toys," Selena remarked while Lydia showed off her collection. Lydia's favorites included two dozen of the tiny Kinder toys that came packaged inside a chocolate egg. Every time Selena picked up her remittances, she bought Lydia an egg.

Turning to the topic of house-building, Selena explained that during his first year abroad, "le fue bien," things went well for Lázaro, and he regularly sent money. Selena got started on a spacious cement-block house by hiring a stonemason. Later, Lázaro's remittances grew sporadic. Construction on the house stopped altogether when Lázaro was unemployed for a stint. At this point, the couple decided to take a cheaper route to independent living. Adjacent to the unfinished structure, they started a two-room, wooden-plank house. Selena hired her father at a discounted rate to carry out the work. (By sharing remittances, migrant wives discovered their parents and siblings appreciated them in ways they never did before.)

By the time Lydia was four years old, the wooden house was nearly complete, but Lázaro was sending only enough to cover basic expenses. Selena had been selling bottled water from her home and was experimenting with cosmetics sales to expand her income and achieve her dream.

Selena wanted to trust her husband, but she was not entirely convinced Lázaro was telling the truth about his earnings. "Has it been raining in Alabama?" she once asked me out of the blue. Roofers cannot work in the rain, and the chief reason many men gave for not sending money was rain. The weather had not been cooperating, they said, so there was less work. Selena knew I often spoke with other wives whose husbands were roofing alongside

Lázaro. She pressed me on any news those women had to share: Had they spoken with their husbands? What did they say about the weather in Alabama?

Keen to live with her husband and daughter in the wooden house, Selena was thinking of advancing the matter by making the move with Lydia. But she saw problems with her plan. The house lacked furniture; it had no stove or refrigerator. Selena's mother had been quiet up to this point in our conversation and now interjected an opinion. Neither a stove nor a refrigerator was necessary, she observed, because Selena knew how to cook over a fire. Most Calakmul housewives fed their families beans and soups that were boiled to prevent spoilage. Watching Selena's dismay at this idea, I sensed that having endured her husband's emigration she might feel a house with a cook fire kitchen was something of a defeat.

More important, there was the crucial subject of Selena's honor. Living without a chaperone opened Selena to accusations of impropriety. Selena's mother was playing devil's advocate with her comment about cooking. As I also learned that afternoon, Selena's mother might have been more concerned about Selena's reputation than Selena was herself. Selena had carefully guarded her reputation for four years, and by living alone in the wooden house, she risked losing the stature she had painstakingly cultivated. To live on her own, Selena had to find a path that met both her economic ideals and her ideal of married life.

Women like Selena epitomized the model migrant wife. Careful with money, she remained firmly ensconced in her family while following her husband's directions. She avoided any behavior that might create suspicions of infidelity. As this chapter explains, women like Selena were models because they embodied two sets of ideals.

One set focused on economics. Calakmuleños had very specific ideas about how migrant families should spend their earnings. Before international migration, few Calakmuleños had reliable access to money. Money flowed within families along gendered and generational lines. The cash that accompanied migration both changed the direction of these flows and gave Calakmuleños the chance to enact models of financial success that had been previously constrained within their repertoires.

The second set of ideals focused on gender and how wives and husbands should behave while a man was abroad. Just as they had with rules against conversation between members of the opposite sex, Calakmuleños placed greater responsibility on young women to fulfill this ideal. Mothers-in-law, gossipy neighbors, and in Selena's case her own mother, saw it as their job to make sure that young women maintained standards.

The two sets of ideals conflicted in ways few women could finesse quite the way Selena did. The conflict centered on a clash between the gender *roles* and the gender *rules* that also formed part of Calakmuleños' repertoire. Gender is the social construction of womanhood and manhood, and people learn these constructions in family settings.[2] In Calakmul, as in other places, men and women were supposed to take on certain roles (that is, behave in certain ways) as a reflection of the rules (the beliefs and norms) associated with their gender. Also, like all cultural groups, Calakmuleños prioritized certain gender expressions, valuing some expressions of masculinity and femininity over others.

With men's departures, family members were forced to change their gender roles. Young wives acquired new skills and took on new habits, especially when they went about spending remittances to enact Calakmuleños' model of success. Financial success was the chief enjoyment Calakmuleños associated with migration. Yet as young wives traveled outside the home and interacted with men outside the family, they broke rules that valued a submissive, socially retiring femininity. The women entered treacherous social terrain where community censure could be intense.

Despite this incongruity, Calakmul's active stayers were hesitant to change either their economic ideals or their gender norms. Changing their economic ideals might mean giving up on their hopes for a better life. Changing their genders norms would mean reshaping their families in profound ways.[3]

Instead, during migration's earliest years, senior women sought to maintain the family as they knew it. They took on the job of "kin keepers," or custodians and enforcers of the kinship rules.[4] The job grew in urgency given the threat migration posed to family ties.[5] Senior women saw it as their duty to ensure that young wives adhered to both economic and gender ideals, regardless of the costs.

FIGURE 4.1
This young woman cared for her four children and the family farm during the five years her husband worked in Alabama. With their husbands in the United States, wives throughout Calakmul were forced to acquire new gender roles. Researchers call women's assumption of farm duties the "feminization of agriculture" (Deere 2005).
Photo: Nora Haenn

Financial Management: Gendered and Generational

One reason for the insistence on premigratory gender norms was that, for senior women and for Calakmuleños in general, the very idea that a young woman like Selena would manage her family's finances was quite new. Their repertoire left Calakmuleños largely unprepared for this possibility. In premigratory Calakmul, family structures discouraged young wives' access to cash. For younger and older women alike, access to money hinged on their generational position in the family. Both generations of women relied on the willingness of the men in their lives to share their earnings. A young wife was especially marginalized when it came to securing money, since patrilocal residence meant her husband's earnings often went to his mother.

To understand why this was the case, it is helpful to start with the financial accord under which many couples in the senior generation operated.

In premigratory Calakmul, marital rules did not require that a husband share money with his wife. Given the value placed on a housebound wife, men tended to take on the chores that entailed leaving the house and spending money. Food shopping was a man's task, as was taking a child to the doctor or purchasing school supplies. Women who undertook these chores tended to do so in the company of their husbands. As a consequence, a husband could adequately care for his family without sharing money with his wife.

This was the general framework in which couples managed their money. Individual couples differed in the precise details of their finances, details that changed as the relationship evolved. Nonetheless, given this outline, some wives felt they could not ask their husbands for money. These women often found themselves forced to manage their households as best they could. To some extent, the accord between spouses that kept men's money separate from women had its merciful side. The bargain allowed poor men, which included most men in Calakmul, to save face. It protected a husband and father from the humiliation of admitting his ability to support his wife and children was limited at best.

At the same time, the bargain was a key component of patriarchal authority. Men could use their money to be mobile, while women were stuck at home. Men found it culturally acceptable to withhold information about how much they earned and where they spent their cash. As elsewhere in Mexico, withholding financial information "increased men's ability to spend . . . on personal pleasures, if they were so inclined."[6] And one area where men might choose to spend their money was extramarital liaisons.

In a few cases, men with the income to do so might support a second woman who behaved as a wife to him. Usually the two women lived at sufficient distance to allow the man to hide his infidelity from his first wife. Whisper campaigns made his infidelity detectable and advertised his ability to afford two households.

These second marriages mixed emotional and monetary giving in complex ways. The second marriages were often part of a "sexual economy," one in which men financially supported women "in exchange for their sexual, reproductive and caring attentions."[7] The arrangements were not merely self-interested. Couples displayed real feelings of affection. For all people, the give and take of gifts creates and maintains relationships by recognizing and giving life to an emotional bond. In Calakmul, people saw that love could grow from a man's spending.

Second marriages were not common in Calakmul, but they took place frequently enough that Calakmuleños assumed a man with disposable income was susceptible to straying. He could easily find a woman to woo with gifts that brought her relief from her own poverty.

It was frustrating for wives, but husbands faced few penalties in spending on themselves while publicly maintaining the fiction that their support for their families was adequate.[8] In reality, many families appeared to be supported only because wives were picking up the slack. Wives usually compensated for the lack of income by making do with less. Then, once a woman's son began to earn money of his own, a new income stream might become available to her.

Sons in Calakmul were not required to give their mothers money, but the pressures to do so were considerable.[9] Mothers expected their sons to be grateful for their sacrifices. Sons absorbed this message and often described the cash they slipped to their mothers as *una ayuda*, a small help meant to alleviate their mothers' burdens. One young man, also a roofer in Alabama, told me he sent money to his mother because he recalled watching her struggle to care for him. His mother was still raising young children (the migrant's brothers and sisters), so this son felt particularly moved to help his mother cover day-to-day expenses. For women accustomed to husbands who earned little or who withheld what cash they did acquire, a son's support offered relief from chronic financial insecurity.

In the era before international migration, these gendered and generational flows continued when a young man married and brought his bride to live in patrilocal residence. Under the norms of patrilocal residence, a daughter-in-law depended on her in-laws for her needs. Thus, after marrying, a young man typically continued to support his mother as manager of the larger household, to whom his wife was accountable. He might divert a portion of his income to his wife while still recognizing his mother as the household's financial administrator.

From a mother's standpoint, a son's marriage marked a turning point in her access to her son's income. Marriage often spurred young men to work, and a mother could benefit financially in the short run from a son's matrimony. Yet in the long run, a son's grownup responsibilities (and grownup pleasures) risked outweighing his mother's needs and leaving her penniless, again.

One assessment of the family violence that mothers-in-law inflicted on daughters-in-law pins the phenomenon on this insecurity. Older women feared penury in their old age. To pressure a son to care for her, a mother might pit her son against his wife by inciting arguments that asked him to choose between his wife and his mother. A mother might coax a son to punish his wife over perceived slights in the interest of reminding him "she has cared for him well his whole life. Her care for him obligates him to care for her in her old age, whether or not the daughter-in-law agrees."[10]

From a young woman's standpoint, a husband's support of his mother hindered the couple's ability to be independent from her in-laws. The less money a young man gave his mother, the more he could direct to building a house of his own, and the faster the couple could make the transition to autonomy. In this way, residential independence was intertwined with financial independence for the young couple, although for young wives, life in a separate residence might mean continued austerity. A separate house might free a daughter-in-law from having to live with her mother-in-law. But if her husband declined to form a financial partnership with her, or if he chose to use his earnings for his own pleasure, a woman might wait until her own sons were grown and employed to gain reliable access to men's earnings.

These family structures meant that, during the years a young couple lived in patrilocal residence, a mother-in-law and daughter-in-law held competitive claims to a young man's earnings. They had different reasons for wanting the money. Deeply disadvantaged in her marriage, the senior woman might view a son's income as overdue compensation for all she had suffered and her only chance for security in old age. A woman's son was her principal hope for respite from grinding poverty. For the younger woman, her husband's income sped the path to independent living. A husband's financial decisions could liberate a young wife from patrilocal residence and give her the chance to run her own home in her own way. Alternatively, his decisions could prolong the time during which a young wife labored under her mother-in-law's direction.

Learning to Be a Model Wife

Having avoided patrilocal residence, Selena eluded any competition with her mother-in-law for Lázaro's earnings. I often wondered how much of Selena's ability to be a model wife was due to her living situation. Selena had sidestepped the many traps young wives of emigrant men unwittingly walked into.

Operating under the assumption that financial managem
continued to fall within their family role during a son's emigration
mothers-in-law across Calakmul scrutinized their daughters-in-law's
every action. Daughters-in-law who managed to maintain residential
independence in sight of their husband's families were especially vulnerable. The senior women accused their daughters-in-law of wasteful
spending. Mothers claimed they were only protecting a son's interests
when they telephoned their sons in the United States to report, "Your
wife went shopping" or "Your wife has taken a trip to the city" or "Your
wife is gone again." Yet as they had with men in the past, senior women
assumed a young woman with disposable income was susceptible to infidelity. Their daughters-in-law's household errands, they claimed, were
a cover for extramarital affairs.[11]

Selena had none of a mother-in-law's scrutiny, but the strength of
local gender norms was such that she strove to maintain her standing
as the faithful and frugal wife nonetheless. Selena did this in very specific ways. She reinforced Lázaro's authority over her day-to-day activities, even though he lived two thousand miles away. And she made sure
others knew she was following his direction. Her continuous banter to
Lydia created a fatherly image for the girl, but it also assured listeners
Selena had no intention of being unfaithful.

Sitting with Selena and her mother in the crammed living room,
I learned Selena's notions of a model migrant wife were partly rooted
in powerful family lore. As a kin keeper herself, Selena's mother had a
stock of morality tales that helped Selena keep to strict principles. Unlike
other Calakmuleños who were new to international travel, members of
Selena's family had been involved in migration for several generations.
Selena grew up hearing stories of philandering emigrant husbands and
morally upright stay-at-home wives.

Selena's mother shared one of these stories, speaking in the rapid-
fire delivery typical of her home state of Veracruz:

> My father was a real womanizer. He had six children with his
> first wife. He was dating my mother when he had two children
> in the United States. My mother knew about the other children,
> but she was just a woman. What could she do?

Selena's grandfather had his US children while working as a *brace*
or guest worker. The Bracero Program was a joint US-Mexico ini
tive that lasted from 1942 to 1964. In all, the program facilitated the

.nporary travel of some two million Mexican laborers to the United .tates.[12] Largely limited to men, the Bracero Program created predictable consequences when it came to people like Selena's grandfather. Whenever husbands and wives are separated for years, the spouses often seek out new partners, if only for the time being. As such, infidelity might be thought of as a byproduct of global economies which, by definition, value workers who are movable.[13]

Other men in Selena's family had also migrated and had been unfaithful to their wives, for which Selena and her mother had a simple explanation: The men were louses. As for the women they hooked up with, Selena and her mother agreed that US women have a special liking for Mexican men and chase after them without consideration for their families in Mexico. The wives who remained in Mexico, they said, were the real victims in all this.

A wife rarely knew the extent of a husband's dalliances. However, one telltale sign of infidelity was a slowdown in the flow of remittances. When an emigrant man began to spend on a new woman, he sent less money home. At her age, Selena's mother cheekily pronounced, she was no longer financially dependent on a man and would not tolerate infidelity: "I'd say get out! You can't come here anymore! My children can dress and feed themselves. So go stay with your gringa. Let her support you." And if a man dared to bring a second wife into the picture: "Nobody is going to push me aside in my house, because in my house, I make the rules."

Still, Selena's mother insisted that younger women live by a different set of rules. A young wife should maintain her honor throughout her husband's absence and remain committed to the marriage.

I ventured a question to Selena's mother, cautiously and as gently as I could. Indirectly, we were talking about Selena's own situation, and for Selena the conversation must have been a sensitive one. I saw now that Selena's bookkeeping along with her repeated requests for Lázaro's permission were meant to send the message that she was holding up .er end of the relationship. By implication, she hoped he was doing the .me, although she could not be entirely sure he was. Migration creates .tubborn information gap between those who migrate and those who .not.[14] The talk of a slowdown in remittances shed light on all those .stions about the weather in Alabama. Selena was trying to gauge .'ther it was really raining or whether another woman had entered th.icture.[15]

Glancing at Selena's photo shopped portrait of her, Lydia, and Lázaro, the question I put to Selena's mother was whether a woman left alone could be tempted by infidelity. The answer was basically yes, although this is not what Selena's mother actually said. Instead, her response was worded in a way that premised the senior generation's warning to young wives. To the question of whether a woman left alone could be tempted by infidelity, Selena's mother said, "If she's honorable, then she will take care of herself, on her own."

As a follow-up, Selena's mother explained, a migrant wife who cheated on her husband might find that when he returned, he would decide to leave her altogether. Unlike an older woman who no longer needed a man, a young wife lacked security. Her husband could return, invoke his patriarchal authority, and take away her house. He might also take away her children.[16]

Financial Success Calakmuleño-Style

With their husbands abroad, young wives like Selena were expected to stick to Calamkuleños' strict gender rules, all while they realized some fairly clear-cut financial goals. As they did with gender roles, Calamkuleños recognized there were obstacles to achieving their financial ideals. But they viewed these obstacles as eminently surmountable. Given the wealth available in the United States, people said, there was no reason a family couldn't transform a man's sojourn into a life of financial autonomy. No reason, that is, unless one or both of the couple fell prey to personal weakness. By sticking to prescribed gender roles— as Selena had—a couple avoided personal weakness and spent remittances correctly to "*sacar en adelante*" the migrant family, literally "pull the family ahead."

Calakmuleños did not give their economic ideal a name, but over time I came to think of it as comparable to the American Dream. Calakmuleños avowed that prosperity comes from hard work and determination, an ideal shared by many people north of the US-Mexico border. Just as people in the United States do, Calakmuleños measured progress in life through financial earnings and the spending this money allowed. They viewed people who climbed the social ladder through migration as upstanding, ethical individuals. Also like their US counterparts, Calakmuleños downplayed the hurdles people faced in making their dreams come true, blaming individuals for failing to best the daunting odds[17]

Calakmuleños' ideas of progress, however, were particular to them. More than anything, by "pulling a family ahead" Calakmul's active stayers emphasized migration was a way out of small-scale farming.

At least two-thirds of county residents were campesinos when international migration got under way.[18] Yet the larger Mexican society did not value this work. To the contrary, upper- and middle-class Mexicans have long viewed campesinos as holding back the country's advancement.[19] Since the passage of NAFTA, Mexico has been committed to supporting food imports and large-scale industrial agriculture. These policies "worsened the conditions of many smallholder agriculturalists."[20] And Calakmuleños took note. By and large, they saw little reason to invest in the job at which most county residents were skilled.

Instead, according to local popular opinion, remittances should be spent to advance other economic plans. Remittances could be used to build a house, as Selena did because young people at her stage in life were expected to seek a residence of their own. "Houses *are* the social relations of those who live in them," and a new house could serve as a "placeholder" for the absent man, a visible sign that he still participated in family life.[21] A woman who successfully oversaw a house's completion advertised her domesticity and her thriftiness in money management.[22] Selena was clearly building a home meant to stand out from its campesino equivalents. Thus, by building her house, Selena moved her family up the social ladder.

Better still than building a house, people said women like Selena should buy ranchland and stock the ranch with cattle. Alternatively, a migrant wife could open a mom-and-pop shop, the kind Calakmuleños commonly ran out of the corner of their home. Selena had done so by selling bottled water. (In yet another global twist, the junk food staples at mom-and-pop shops were typically made by global corporations and laden with imported high fructose corn syrup.)[23] Remittances might also be used to support children's education, with the goal that youngsters avoid a life of manual labor altogether. Education, people believed, gave youngsters access to *un trabajo sentado*, "a sit-down job," or what we in the United States might call a "desk job."

The cattle ranch, mom-and-pop shop, and children's education were for Calakmuleños a financial mantra, a formula repeated by senior women and junior women alike. It didn't matter much that the region experienced droughts every three years or so, and some communities had no water to support large animals. It also did not matter much that smaller villages could sustain only so many shops, or that a child's education was no guarantee of economic security. Unemployment rates for young people in Mexico tend to be two and three times that of older adults, with higher rates affecting people with high school and university educations.[24]

The formula was popular because it pointed to the shared social norms that Calakmuleños valued.[25] Active stayers said migrant couples should stick with these goals. Migrant couples should do so by sacrificing short-term comfort in order to maximize the money earned abroad. Curtailing their spending to the extent possible, continuing to live as austerely as campesinos had in the past, migrant families should, as the saying went, eat "little more than beans."

What were the shared norms behind these investment goals? Notably, the jobs that Calakmuleños prized all required less physical labor than farming, with the sit-down job exemplifying a leisurely, salaried life. Calakmuleños clearly valued using migration to lighten their load.

The list also stressed self-employment. Although they wanted to get out of farming, there was one aspect of smallholding life Calakmuleños did not want to abandon. In their farming, campesinos managed their own time and did not take direction from a supervisor. Their migration ideals continued to accentuate this freedom. Calakmuleños wanted to work independently in a lucrative line of business.

For women, the family-run shop offered dignified working conditions that eluded most people in the region. If Calakmuleños agreed on anything, it was that their local job market was unfriendly to workers. The lack of appealing situations posed particular challenges to women. Campesinas tended to qualify for jobs as cooks or waitresses at eateries in the county seat. Campesinas also filled the ranks of housekeepers, domestic servants, or menial laborers in one of the region's larger family-owned shops.[26] These positions usually demanded schedules of ten- to twelve-hour days, six days a week, all for a wage of about $14 a day. For a woman with a young child, the schedule made it impossible to cover her duties at home. Selena, for example, did not consider looking for one of these jobs, although she needed the cash.

In addition to the jobs' low pay, the stringent hours placed a boss front and center in workers' lives. Bosses who threw their weight around without cause were a common complaint. When I asked migrant men who had returned from the United States how Calakmul employers differed from their US counterparts, the men invariably shared that US bosses were easier on workers. It was a difference that defied words. Illustrating the demands of a typical Calakmul boss, the men gave a hurried snapping of their fingers that translated into "get hopping, get moving." Calakmul employers could be unrelenting because an overall dearth of jobs meant an underling who complained was easily replaced.

Honorable, homebound wives like Selena sought protection from such shabby treatment. Yet even if a woman reconciled herself to low pay, long hours, and an overbearing boss, she was very likely to run into her husband's objections. Men, who were concerned for their own honor, felt shame in having a working wife. A man with an income-earning wife could no longer maintain the fiction that his support for his family was adequate. (An exception was the wife with a sit-down job, whose pay might be enough to bring a family prestige.) His neighbors would gossip that his wife used her time outside the house to cheat on him. A working wife doubly embarrassed a man by making him appear to be a destitute cuckold.

These work-related gender dynamics meant that an entrepreneurial woman like Selena had few options. If she wanted to earn an income, she needed to do so in a way that allowed her to remain within the confines of the family. She needed a family-centered business, something like a mom-and-pop store. In order to get one, she needed start-up funds, and these were scarce in Calakmul. From this perspective, the advent of international migration offered Calakmuleños a rare opportunity. Migration gave active stayers—and especially the region's women—the chance to "pull the family ahead" by enacting a gendered economic ideal that was previously unattainable.

The path to attaining this dream was always hazardous. A wife like Selena had to carefully advertise her adherence to old gender norms. She did so all the while she broke those same norms by becoming an active, mobile, economic agent.

Given the pressures on migrant wives, Selena's independent move into her clapboard house was nothing short of a triumph. She pulled off the move after her repeated attempts at securing gender-appropriate financial security failed. The bottled-water sales offered a little income, but not enough to cover the costs of appliances and furniture. The cosmetics sales restricted her interactions to other women, but stiff competition and company policies that required her to enter a minimum monthly order quickly undid her efforts. Selena also went to considerable lengths to meet her mother's expectation that she live with a chaperone. She contacted one of Lázaro's nephews, who lived two hours away, and asked the youngster if he would consider moving. He decided to remain with his parents.

In the end, Selena managed to persuade Lázaro to give her permission to make the move. Selena's mother was unhappy with the decision, but given her insistence that a young wife cede to her husband's authority, she could hardly object. Lázaro's approval was also key to furnishing the house. With his go-ahead, Selena purchased a stove, refrigerator, washing machine, and furniture. She had to buy some things on credit, but she had the complete set. Her shopping had the effect of expanding migration's global reach. While men's travels constituted one globalization in Calakmul, women's spending on consumer items connected the region to global food systems, as well as manufacturers in China, Japan, and Mexico's largest trading partner, the United States. Where cook fires on raised platforms went hand-in-hand with locally grown food, kitchens built around imported refrigerators and gas stoves were more amenable to processed foods—the sugary yogurts, prefabricated salsas, and other foods sold in mom-and-pop shops—the sort of food made increasingly available by trade deals like NAFTA.[27]

Soon after her move into the wooden house, I visited with Selena to see how things were going. The stove was still in its original box and the refrigerator wrapped in plastic. Her new home was as crammed as her parents' living room, but everything was hers. Plus all the expensive belongings gave Selena a respectable explanation for living unsupervised. Selena lived in a town that has long had problems with thieves, but they rarely entered an occupied home. Selena and Lydia needed to spend as much time as possible at the house to make sure nothing was stolen.

The home's construction was still incomplete; the bath needed finishing. Selena and Lydia had to walk the four blocks to Selena's mother's house every day to wash up. But the bother was worth it. Selena spent her time making small improvements around the place in anticipation of Lázaro's arrival. After five long years, he *said he was finally coming home, and Selena was anxious to have everything just right.*

I next saw the family a few years later, and they seemed the picture of domestic contentment. Lázaro had, indeed, come home soon after Selena secured her independence. I suspect one of the reasons Selena was so insistent on moving was to force his return. As long as Selena continued to live with her mother, Lázaro did not have to worry about her so much. As a supposedly vulnerable wife, living alone after achieving the couple's dream, Selena could press more forcefully for Lázaro's homecoming.

If this had been Selena's idea, the plan worked. When I visited, I greeted a ten-year-old Lydia, who now shared her parents' attention with two younger brothers.

The family was still living in that two-room wooden house, overflowing with stuff for five people. To supplement the family income, Selena ran a mom-and-pop store out of a corner of one of the rooms. She sold cookies, crackers, potato chips, sodas, and other snacks, and paid for stock with revolving credit from one of the new banks that opened in the wake of migration's increased cash flow. Selena managed the store while caring for her children and attending to her household duties.

Selena told me that while the store did not cover all the family's expenses, it offered some help. The shop was successful enough that it also inspired envy in her neighbor a few doors down, a woman whose own mini-market predated Selena's. Selena found evidence for the jealousy in a mishap that befell her while walking around her yard. Selena tripped and damaged her Achilles' tendon. The injury was taking months to heal, and Selena was convinced her spiteful neighbor used witchcraft to cause the accident.

The block house Selena and Lázaro had begun to build ten years earlier loomed skeletal, in the middle of the property. Its walls were shoulder-height in parts, waist-high in others. Cutouts awaited doors and windows. Rebar poked out at odd angles from the masonry. Occasionally, Selena and Lázaro had to clear the weeds sprouting up through the concrete floor.

There had never been enough money to finish construction. Upon his return, Lázaro took the building skills he honed in the United States and found work as a stonemason putting up *cement-block homes for other migrant families and the recipients of state-run housing programs. Construction work paid $35 a day, roughly equivalent to the take-home pay for a minimum-wage worker in the United States but half the amount Lázaro had earned as a roofer in Alabama. Lázaro's earnings allowed the couple to complete the wooden house, but there were times between building projects when Lázaro was unemployed.*

Money often ran low, forcing Selena to cut costs by forgoing gas to fuel the cook stove. Instead, Selena made the family's meals over a fire on a raised platform that Lázaro had built in the corner of the family's yard where the wooden and cement-block houses formed a perpendicular line. Selena cooked in a campesina's kitchen. But her family was together and growing, and all in all she did not seem to mind the kitchen.

Notes

1. About fifteen years after migration from Calakmul got underway, the Mexican government had established libraries with internet service in villages throughout the region. The internet gave migrants and their families access to low cost and confidential communication in the form of Whatsapp and Facebook.
2. See Collier and Yanagisako 1987. Some societies recognize additional genders beyond this simple binary, see Davies 2007.
3. Pribilsky 2007
4. Reeder 2003.
5. Citing Akpinar, Brettell 2017 notes that women in migratory settings often play the role of bearers of group identity. Given the stigma of Indigenous identity, Calakmuleños emphasized gender ideals moreso than ethnic identities.
6. Hondagneu-Sotelo 1994: 69.
7. Cole 2010: 73. See also Constable 2009; Hannaford 2017. On gifts and relationships, see Mauss 2002 (1925); Wilk and Cliggett 2007.
8. See also Levine and Correa 1993.
9. Elsewhere in Mexico, women were more frank about their demands. Working in Oxcutzcab, a town a few hours north of Calakmul, Alison Greene had the mother of an emigrant son in Cancún say that if her son didn't deliver on the money, she would grab her baseball bat and go looking for him. I thank Alison for sharing this story.
10. McClusky 2001: 254.

11. There were a few ways men's migration required wives to travel. Women living in rural communities traveled to the county seat to collect their remittances and, in the years before cell and internet service, speak with their husbands on the phone. The men typically scheduled phone calls on Sundays, a day that was both traditional and, for many, their only reliable day off. Offices where women cashed in the remittances where only open Monday through Saturday.

12. Cohen 2011: 2. For more on the Bracero program, see: http://braceroarchive.org/.

13. Hirsch et al. 2009: 201.

14. Hannaford 2017: 9.

15. Selena wasn't the only woman asking me this question. During the height of emigration, the weather in Alabama was a trending topic on Calakmul's gossip network.

16. Women's fears of losing their children were not unreasonable. Although women carried out day-to-day caregiving, patriarchal norms gave biological fathers primary responsibility for children (cf. McClusky 2001). In one dispute, a Calakmul magistrate removed a woman's children from her and awarded custody to the woman's former mother-in-law. The children's father lived in the United States, and local observers of the case concluded the judge's decision was based on the fact that the elder woman now received his remittances while the young woman had no reliable income.

17. On social mobility in the United States, Cohen (2019) offers a simple graphic that contrasts the actual possibility of climbing the social ladder with people's optimism about such mobility. Cohen draws on the research of the economist Stefanie Stantcheva who breaks her data down by state. In Alabama, for example, some 4.5% of children whose families ranked in the bottom 20% of income earners both at the child's birth and in the child's second decade of life had moved up to the top 20% of income earners by their 30s. Yet surveys showed Alabamians believed twice as many people had made this leap.

18. INEGI 2010.

19. Cancian 1994; Gálvez 2018; Walker 2013.

20. Fitting 2011: 103.

21. Carsten 2004: 37. James Ferguson (1990) describes cattle in Lesotho as placeholders. He describes investments in cattle by men as creating a tangible reminder of emigrant men's continued participation in family life.

22. Grigolini 2005.

23. Gálvez 2018.

24. OECD 2015; Ruiz Nápoles and Ordáz Díaz 2011.

25. See also Cliggett 2005.
26. Calakmuleños recognized that economic necessity forced women to work. For women, the kind of job mattered. Many Calakmuleña women worked outside the home, in education, health care, and in local government. These middle-class, salaried positions were less stigmatized. Jobs in nursing and education brought prestige to a working woman. By definition, however, middle-class jobs did not tend to be filled by campesina women. The latter found honor in coming from a family that earned enough, a wife did not have to work.
27. See Reeder 2003; Gálvez 2018.

....

CHAPTER 5

Aurora: The Pleasure-Seeking Wife

When I met Aurora in 1994, she was a quiet, well-behaved thir-teen-year-old. I never imagined Aurora would one day be ma-ligned as the scandalous wife of an emigrant. When Aurora was a girl, I visited her family in Orozco nearly every day for eight months while carrying out my research. Invariably, I found the teenager grinding corn for tortillas. Grinding corn was a tiresome job mothers typically offloaded to their daughters as soon as pos-sible. The grinder Aurora worked had a gray steel funnel screwed into a heavy-duty red frame that was clamped onto a table. The grinder's arm turned with a stiff crank, so for about an hour each day, Aurora stood rocking back and forth, throwing her whole body into the exercise. Aurora's labor freed her mother to care for a family that included ten children. Aurora's father worked as a farmer and village official. Both parents were strong-minded and determined to improve their family's circumstances. Yet this attitude did not keep them from pulling Aurora out of school after she repeatedly failed the fourth grade. Her parents decided Aurora's time was better spent working at home.

Aurora's mother, Chavela, derived her parenting philosophy from her own stint in patrilocal residence. Chavela said she was purposefully hard on her daughters in order to prepare them for life with a mother-in-law. Chavela had married at thirteen and took a beating whenever her mother-in-law decided her housekeeping was lacking. Chavela said she wanted to spare her daughters the same treatment, so, in effect, she held her daughters to her mother-in-law's unreasonable standards. It must be said that Chavela's daughters did not quite see the benefit to this education. When I met Aurora, her eighteen-year-old sister had already run off to the city. Aurora would marry her husband, Juan Diego, and move out of the house at age fourteen.

By the time Aurora was twenty-eight, her husband had traveled abroad, and Calakmul's rumor mill was abuzz with talk of her behavior. While Chavela was ultimately proved right—Aurora's mother-in-law influenced the young woman's life profoundly—the gossipers focused on Aurora herself.

I first heard her story while sitting with a group of Ch'ol friends from Orozco. They were catching me up on village news, and for my benefit, the conversation was in Spanish. When we got to the topic of travel to the United States, my friend Benito took the floor. Benito had never migrated, but he had strong opinions about the endeavor. One of his cousins, he pronounced, had been so wasteful with her husband's money that when the migrant returned home thinking there would be 10,000 dollars "stuffed in the blanket," he discovered only half that amount. On the topic of migrant men, "Those guys come back, and they're walking around like they're hot stuff. They say they speak English, but all you ever hear out of them are curse words when they get drunk." I do not think Benito noticed when he switched from Spanish to Ch'ol. Whatever he was talking about was apparently so shameful, it required a more intimate idiom. I heard him mention the names of Aurora and Juan Diego. When the conversation seemed to focus on Aurora, there were gasps of disbelief when Benito said something about a taxi driver and something about a cantina.

"For me, this is the saddest case," Benito shared when we got around to a translation. According to him, when Juan Diego went to the United States, Aurora and the couple's three children moved in with her family. Aurora did not live with her in-laws because Juan Diego identifies as Ch'ol, and his parents speak only the Indigenous language. Aurora speaks only Spanish. Juan Diego and Aurora lived next door to both sets of parents, so in order to fulfill the ideal that she have male protection and chaperones to vouch *for her honor, Aurora relocated about fifty yards away. She re-mained close enough to her in-laws for them to keep an eye on her.*

"But what happened?" Benito could not hide his disap-proval. Juan Diego reportedly sent about $200 a week. "Every week Aurora and her family sat down at the table playing cards," he mimed dealing hands for poker. "In the center of the table, they had bottles and bottles of beer. Every week. That's where the money went." Again, according to Benito, Juan Diego sent word from the United States that he wanted a house built, and his fa-ther-in-law promised to do the job. The timber was readied for construction, but somehow the project never got off the ground. The rest of the money was spent elsewhere, and the timber was sold or given away.

When Juan Diego returned to Mexico, there was no new construction and no money saved, and he was humiliated to find his wife working in a cantina. In Calakmul, it goes without saying that cantina waitresses have a second, more lucrative job offering sex for sale. Thus, Benito's audience was horrified upon hearing that when Juan Diego saw his wife for the first time in two years, she was serving beer. The taxi driver was supposedly her new boyfriend.

Because in my mind, I remembered a girlish Aurora rocking back and forth at that corn grinder, it was hard to picture her as a dissolute wife. And because public gossip can be very different from people's private reality, it made sense to ask Aurora if she would share her version of the story. Was she really acting out of a sense of abandonment or was something more going on here? I also sought out Juan Diego's viewpoint. At the least, I hoped to solve the mystery of how the couple ever managed to marry. Au-rora's parents hardly let her leave the house. From what I could tell, Aurora's life was so restricted, she never had the chance to speak with her husband before marrying him. What had mar-riage meant to Aurora at its start? And now that her husband had migrated and returned home, what did marriage mean to the grown up Aurora?

Calakmuleños gave migrant wives a telling nickname. They called the women "Black Widows." Model migrant wives were sup-posed to conduct themselves as if in mourning. During their husbands' absence, and atop all their other newly acquired duties, wives of emigrant men were supposed to carry out a very specific kind of emotional labor. Yet the nickname also hinted at the danger this new status posed. Widows are eligible to remarry. As women who were married yet alone, migrant wives might break up the family by allowing strangers to enter into it. The exemplary wife responded to this danger, as Selena had, by maintaining vigilant guard over her person and her money. Her disreputable counterpart became the target of gossip. Tongues wagged about wives who supposedly spent their husband's earnings frivolously. The most scandalous women stood accused of using remittances to finance their extramarital affairs.

In this chapter we hear from Aurora, an allegedly disgraced wife. We also hear from her husband, Juan Diego. Together, the couple show that Calakmuleños' stereotypes regarding migration's pleasures and dangers failed to capture the gender changes under way. Before international migration, Calakmuleños tended to value female self-abnegation. With the advent of international travel, wives began to learn new skills and develop new identities that were "increasingly independent of their husband's patriarchal control."[1] As part of these changes, young people went about revising gender norms to emphasize personal fulfillment and consumerism.

A new generation of marriage partners expected their relationships to be built on romance and emotional compatibility rather than the shared workload of farming.[2] Young people viewed these qualities as modern. Indeed, the appearance of love-based marriages in many parts of the world has suggested to some researchers that they are part of globalization's emotional landscape.[3] Romance and emotional support were qualities Calakmul's senior generation may have hoped for but did not expect.

Aurora and Juan Diego's example illustrates how migration's pleasures and dangers, with their attendant ideas of romance and consumerism, were bound up with one another. In her study of migration and sexuality, the sociologist Gloria González-López finds pleasure and danger co-existing on a single continuum. Sexuality is "a malleable process in constant flux," she writes.[4] Its pleasures and dangers blend into one another, such that people can easily slip back and forth between enjoyment and peril. Because Calakmuleños viewed travel, spending, and sex as part of a single package, the pleasure-danger continuum they associated with migration was more expansive than one that focused on sex alone. In all these areas, Calakmuleños found it hard to assure personal fulfillment without also running the risk of personal distress.

Part of the underlying tension was that older gender ideals, as well as long-standing gender relations, did not simply disappear. Instead, the adoption of migratory-related pleasures and dangers was uneven across Calakmul. Some women felt burdened by having to take on men's roles. These women found migration expanded their household duties, and they wished to return to the marriages they had before migration.[5] In contrast, women like Aurora, who pursued novel gendered identities, found themselves in jeopardy of social condemnation.

In any cultural setting, gender and family ideals unavoidably disadvantage those who, for one reason or another, do not live up to the standards. Women like Aurora faced a particular kind of challenge when it came to living up to older and new standards alike. To achieve the personal fulfillment migration promised, they had to expand the local repertoire and claim privileges formerly denied to wives.

Aurora and her peers soon learned they had few socially acceptable routes by which to pursue migration's pleasures. At this point, it is important to note that gender ideals are not always hard-and-fast. Gender and kinship frameworks typically include opportunities for individuals to break with norms in ways that are frowned on but are, at minimum, socially acceptable.[6] In post-migratory Calakmul, men's pathways to new gendered identities included breaking rules in socially acceptable ways. Breaking rules was a privilege Calakmuleños already ascribed to men. Women were not accorded the same leeway. By seeking her own enjoyment or, as we see with Aurora, by defending herself when migration threatened to end her marriage, a woman breached norms stipulating a wife without her husband should live a joyless bereavement. The kin keepers among her neighbors and in-laws invoked the older standards and pressured wives like Aurora to comply.

Changing Pleasures and Dangers in Calakmul

Migratory-related pleasures and dangers took place against a backdrop of broader transformations. As the twenty-first century got under way, young people across Calakmul began to participate in "youth culture."[7] Under the old agrarian order, young people married in their teens, and in one swift moment their status changed from child to adult (albeit junior adult). People's lives as children and adults were not all that different in the sense that all family members were engaged, in one way or another, in farming. In the new century, young people still married in their teens, but many aspects of their lives became distinct from those of their parents.

Increasingly, young Calakmuleños were obsessed with consumer items and the name brands that evoked prosperity. They inspected each other's sneakers for the telltale stitching that said Puma, Converse, or Adidas. Young women handed around catalogs from Fuller cosmetics, Andrea clothing, and Ilusión lingerie. Both women and men rarely left home without their hair coiffed to perfection, preferably with a premium gel that goes by the name Gorilla Snot.

International migration contributed to this growing youth culture both directly and indirectly. Remittances circulating in the local economy allowed for consumer purchases that were previously beyond Calakmuleños' reach. The new stylishness reflected a work ethic that people viewed as one of the goals of migration. Meticulous grooming was hard to maintain working a farm, but it fit well with the sit-down jobs the children of migrants aspired to secure.

Moreover, international migration infused this consumerism with sex. Migration created a heightened sexual atmosphere in Calakmul because families knew that men were likely to be engaging in stateside dalliances. "In Mexico, I'm married—but here I am single," an Atlanta-based man professed to one researcher.[8] Emigrant men did not advertise these exploits. They had effectively agreed that what happens in the United States stays in the United States. However, their wives strongly suspected they were drinking and womanizing, leaving Aurora and women expected to live as Black Widows to bristle at the double standard imposed upon them: "If he's out having a good time in the United States, why shouldn't I do the same here? What's wrong with me going out for fun?"

To get a sense of how sex and consumerism combined to create new marital bargains, consider a wedding ritual that appeared in the years after international migration got under way. It was called *desnudar el novio* or "undressing the groom." The ritual took place during nuptials that included the latest trends: white dresses, wedding cakes, party favors, and a lengthy guest list (Figure 5.1). The costly weddings required yet a new category of kin to pay for them. Cash-strapped couples worked their networks to find "godfathers" and "godmothers" to pay for the drinks and food along with the wedding dress, tableware, and decorations. Weddings became a moment for young couples to display their

FIGURE **5.1**
In the early 2000s, new ideas of romance went hand-in-hand with new wedding rituals in Calakmul. At the time, Calakmul did not have bridal shops, and this groom traveled to a city five hours away to purchase a wedding gown. Unaccustomed to the ritual, we guests all gave the same gift. Each of the gift bags contained a set of dinner plates.
Photo: Nora Haenn

social connections and their plans to live a life replete with the trappings of consumerism. "Undressing the groom" sent the message these marriages would be sexy as well as moneyed.

Here's how the ritual went: As the wedding reception was winding down and the wedding night drew near, the groom's friends carried him out of the party. They removed all his clothes, soaped him up, and gave him a scrubbing. The friends then returned to the party to collect the bride, who, laughing and blushing, was presented with her new husband, washed naked of any impurities he might have brought to the marriage. Men's premarital sexual encounters in Mexico often entailed peer pressure to make it appear as though a young man could not be blamed for breaking the taboo on premarital sex.[9] In the ritual, the groom and his pals acknowledged the importance of sex in building camaraderie among men. Meanwhile, expectations that young women be chaste remained intact. At least one Calakmul-area church required a doctor's medical exam of brides to prove they deserved a virginal white dress.

With their peers enjoying innovations like "undressing the groom," few wives of emigrant men wanted to enter a period of mourning. At the same time, for all the women in this younger generation, the new pleasure-danger continuum left open a crucial question: Just what would women's post-marital pleasures look like? "Undressing the groom" showed that Calakmuleños' changing ideas of marriage still held conflicting expectations of men and women before marriage. The ritual also suggested a sexual ambiguity at the heart of the new marital bargain. Was the groom's cleansing permanent, or would the friends be carousing together in the future? Were the groom's friends handing the husband over to the bride, or were they inviting the bride into a sanitized version of a sexualized world built by and for men?

The ordeals faced by migrants' stay-at-home wives placed these ambiguities in stark relief. Remittances from the United States gave Aurora and women like her unique entrée into the consumerism that Calakmuleños increasingly prized. Yet when Aurora and other "Black Widows" sought fulfillment in sex and romance—a fulfillment already accorded to men—they ran up against persistent double standards.

Gossip at Aurora and Juan Diego's House

The penalty women like Aurora faced mainly entailed gossip. The pressure could be intense, as one target of a rumor campaign wailed: "They talk and talk and talk. You don't know how hard it can be when they start talking!"

Gossip was nothing new to the era of international migration. It was part of Calakmuleños' daily life. After leaving patrilocal residence, young couples often set up house near the man's parents and, in doing so, helped create neighborhood clusters centered on the male line. These neighborhoods were also a kind of "gossip unit," where family life entailed "exposing oneself to the gaze of others . . . [and becoming] the object of gossip."[10] Little about a person's life escaped public attention. Aurora and other Calakmuleños took for granted that their family and neighbors would use gossip to shape what in the United States would be considered a person's private life.

International migration increased the intensity of the chatter. Community gossip aimed at migrant families is common.[11] And cross-culturally, gossip typically centers on cultural ideals that are hard to live up to. Valued norms that, in practice, conflict with social roles also tend to be topics that inspire gossip.[12] As Calakmuleños began to live the conflicts that migration created between gender roles and gender norms, including the way a new generation pressed for normative change, they followed in the steps of migrant families elsewhere and gossiped about married couples.[13]

To understand the gossip about Aurora and Juan Diego, I visited the couple in their sturdy cement-block house, one that would have drawn considerable envy before the building boom that accompanied international migration. The house juts out of the ground, shorn of any nearby vegetation to soften its stark gray lines. Calakmul housekeeping often includes removing shrubbery and grass that might provide cover for rodents, snakes, foxes, and opossums. People cut down the tall trees that hurricane winds turn into battering rams. Crossing the threshold, I saw the stamp in the concrete floor, the seal of the state of Campeche that marked this building as part of a government housing project. The state had paid for the building materials while Juan Diego and Aurora arranged for construction, with Juan Diego putting in the bulk of the labor. While the materials were enviable, the size of the house was limited by what the government was willing to pay. Its single, spartan room contained a double bed, a hammock, a loveseat, a table, and a brand-new armoire, each of its three doors lighting up the darkened space with an inlaid, full-length mirror. A bag of jalapeño chili pepper seeds hung from the rafters, awaiting the next season's planting.

When Aurora and I had the chance to speak alone, I posed the question I usually asked the wives of emigrant men: "What advice would you give to a woman whose husband is about to go to the United States?" Only one woman ever jettisoned conventional wisdom to speak frankly: "You know, I would tell her not to get her hopes up. Because it seems to me it's the same whether they go or not. It would be better if he just stayed at home. My husband doesn't earn much, and the money he sends is the same he could have made here working odd jobs."

Aurora gave the more common, culturally appropriate answer. Aurora is a stout woman with light skin that sets off her wavy black hair. As she sat upright on the hammock, her toes barely reached the floor. The day she and I talked, she was dressed in a black polyester skirt and a yellow blouse that clung to her chubby figure. Her hands folded in her lap, she answered my question with a serious, matronly tone: "I would tell the woman to behave herself, to stay at home and take care of the children. Don't go out. Keep the house fixed up, keep the yard clean, and when he calls, then you have to leave home to speak on the phone."

Orozco's only telephone was located in the house of a village official. "If he doesn't call," Aurora continued, "stay at home. Because when a woman leaves the house, there are problems. People start saying things that are not true, and that's when the husband begins to get the wrong idea."

At first, Aurora avowed that this was what happened to her. She was not a profligate wife but one undone by gossip. As I delved into her and Juan Diego's versions of events, I saw that the gossip leveled against her was powerful because it served the community's larger purposes. Calakmuleños used gossip to discourage or penalize what they viewed as inappropriate gender behavior. But they also used gossip to learn what migration was all about. By relating to a migrant couple the news they had gathered from the rumor mill, active stayers probed the migratory experiences of people undergoing the venture firsthand. Gossipers tested what migration meant for those involved and how far migration's social inventions might be pushed.

Aurora's and Juan Diego's sides of the story also demonstrated how quickly gossip could undermine a marriage. Gossip naturally lent itself to the circulation of multiple, conflicting versions of a story. Usually, when a couple lived in the same place, they could manage the gossip by comparing the different perspectives and weighing them against their personal experience of their spouse. Living two thousand miles apart, Aurora and Juan Diego could not rely on their personal viewpoints. They had to ferret out information the best they could, usually from family members who were themselves spreading rumors for their own purposes. The result was a dangerous game of telephone, with the couple's marriage hanging precariously in the balance. For Aurora and Juan Diego, some parts of their stories proved impossible to reconcile. But the most damaging part of the gossip swirling about them was that much of it was true.

Juan Diego's Side of the Story

Juan Diego was an intense, soft-spoken man, just an inch or two taller than his wife. Like Aurora, he had black hair, but his skin was much darker. Juan Diego sported a mustache barely noticeable against his complexion. His rich, cocoa coloring reflected the hours he spent in his fields, although he much preferred his duties as village official. As one of Orozco's elected leaders, Juan Diego traveled regularly to Calakmul's county seat and elsewhere. The job made him feel socially connected after his return from Texas.

their extravagant spending on personal pleasure, all of these resonated with the clandestine world they shared in Calakmul's cantinas. In fact, active stayers often described the United States as if the country were one big cantina.

In this way, her husband's migration opened the path for Aurora to partake in migration's fun-filled atmosphere. Aurora did not cross an international border, but she did cross the boundary that separated home life from cantina life, the boundary between a life of drudgery and a life of celebration. At first, her journey felt empowering to Aurora, even exhilarating. But she soon faced a backlash and punishment for her pleasure-seeking.

Breaking Gendered Rules

By working at the cantina, Aurora took Calakmul's new pleasure-danger continuum to its logical conclusion and, in doing so, reformulated the continuum. If men could have fun, then so could she. If men could break rules, she could do that, too. But as a waitress, Aurora breached the imaginary line Calakmuleños had drawn not just between home and the cantina but between wives and prostitutes. She tripped on a series of mutually supporting rules meant to hold wives in their place. Interestingly, Aurora's time in the cantina gave her access to men's secret world, and this presumably included the secrets harbored by the husbands of her fellow wives. But this did not seem to be what scandalized the gossipmongers.

Instead, what appeared to shock them was Aurora's willingness to make her marital infidelity visible and thus reveal her dissatisfaction with married life. Calakmuleños assumed women would want to be wives. The honor of being a stay-at-home wife was supposed to compensate a woman for renouncing her own desires in the service of her husband and children. Aurora, and wives like her, reminded observers that married women's desires could not be relinquished entirely, especially when it came to sex.

Over the years, I had heard a few Calakmuleños say that sex was essential to a person's health and well-being. Men's need for sex, they said, arose before they married. As a result, Calakmuleños tolerated men's premarital escapades. After a woman was married and became sexually knowledgeable, people said, her need could be equally strong. On more than one occasion, I noticed that a wife who found herself newly alone—because her husband had died or emigrated, or because the marriage had ended—was quickly approached by fervent suitors who imagined her need for sexual attention made her susceptible to persuasion.

Sexual energy had a will of its own, people said, and underpinned the one marginally acceptable way that both women and men could break the rule on marital fidelity. Overwhelming sexual attraction, people said, might drive a woman or a man to a short-lived extramarital "adventure." Adventures were flings in which desire was supposedly so powerful, the couple could not control themselves. While painful for a cuckolded spouse, these sexual side trips were ultimately forgivable because, for Calakmuleños, people could not be entirely blamed for being caught in the grip. The region's sexual double standard contained a mechanism for managing these breaches. Where a man might brag about such a liaison, a woman certainly would not. In the premigratory era, and despite the vigorousness of gossip networks, both men and women were scrupulously silent on the fact of married women's infidelities.

Aurora's work at the cantina scandalized because she did not hide the fact that she was breaking rules. By working in a party venue, she signaled she was unwilling to deny herself personal fulfillment. She did not care much who knew about her pleasure-seeking life. Then Aurora took one more step in expanding the gendered aspects of Calakmuleños' repertoire: She fell in love.

By definition, the brief flings that stood as women's single, narrow escape from marital confines were not supposed to grow into long-term, caring relationships. Aurora, however, was from a different generation. With her husband gone, she watched as her counterparts among Calakmul's active stayers built marriages on romance and emotional compatibility. As she contemplated a second chance at matrimony, Aurora thought she might achieve the same.

As it turned out, Aurora and Juan Diego's marriage had been a face-saving measure that her parents insisted on. To circumvent the rules that forbade conversation between men and women, the youngsters courted in the midnight hours. Juan Diego waited until all of Orozco was asleep to sneak into Aurora's backyard, a grove of lemon, lime, and orange trees. Aurora joined him by slinking outside her parents' three-room house. Their flirtation

*must not have been completely stealthy. I remember Aurora's
younger sister teasing her about having a boyfriend. It was probably only a matter of time before the relationship became public
knowledge. Soon enough, Aurora's grandfather spied the couple
together. With the secret out in the open, Aurora's parents urged
her to marry.*

*"The truth is," Aurora told me about her time while her hus-
band was abroad, "I did have a boyfriend, but we weren't physical." Aurora spoke of her love when I asked her about a woman's
need for sex: "If a husband goes away and does not say when he'll
return, how long can a wife go without sex?" "Well, the truth is,"
Aurora explained, "a woman doesn't last long without sex."*

*Her boyfriend was the taxi driver she hired to take her to
work at the cantina. "He used to say to me, 'You know, your husband isn't coming back. Why don't you get a divorce, and we can
be together; we can get married.' He said he would speak with my
father to ask for my hand, but I begged him not to. One day, he
came here to the house with a marriage contract he had written
himself, already signed. 'Go on, sign!' he said. I told him I would
think it over and come see him the next day, but I never went. He
was still with his wife, and that's what discouraged me. I thought
to myself, I have my husband and my children. He has his wife
and his four children. To tear apart two homes like that, it's not
so easy."*

*Aurora gave special emphasis to that marriage contract.
Seeing the promise of enduring love in writing made a strong impression on her. I could tell she struggled hard with whether or
not to walk away from Juan Diego. And as with the conflicting
story of Juan Diego and the remittances, Aurora's description of
her love affair left the sequence of events uncertain. Did Aurora
end the relationship with the taxi driver before Juan Diego returned? Or did his sudden reappearance force its conclusion?
In her telling, the sequence was unimportant. What did matter
was that in the end she decided she would remain in her marital
home, holding together both family and gender ideals in the face
of the changes emigration had brought.*

*When I visited with Aurora, she was mainly spending her
time in the cement-block farmer's house. Her place in the cantina had been taken up by Juan Diego. With her husband's return*

from the United States, Aurora had resumed the life of a proper matron. This meant she was seeing less of the musical and romantic side of alcohol that she had known before and more of its violent consequences. Juan Diego hit Aurora when he was drunk.

For his part, Juan Diego said he would not recommend travel to the United States to his own children. He gave the usual reasons most Calakmul parents did, but with a credibility born of personal experience. Juan Diego was deported three times in all, including once from Phoenix when a gunfight broke out between his smugglers and the police were called. "I'll tell my children I know that life," Juan Diego said. "Life in the United States isn't so easy. Yes, you can buy a car. You just go to the agency, show them your pay stub, and set up a payment plan. But you have to work every day of the week. Because the one day you don't work, you don't eat. You have to pay rent, you have to pay water, electricity, all kinds of bills." In Calakmul, other than electricity, there were few charges that must be paid by a specific date. The weight of monthly bills in the United States was such that "bill" was one of the first English words migrant men learned. Their Spanish had no equivalent.

Juan Diego listed weightier reasons why he would advise his children against international migration: "You endanger your life. I'll tell my children that we're poor, but we'll always have food to eat, even if it's just beans. Already I tell them, 'Study hard, so that when you're fifteen, sixteen, eighteen years old, it will be easier to find a job. Go and find that job. Don't risk your life in the desert. The moment you leave home for the United States, you risk your life. Who will stay by you while you lay dying in the desert? If you don't die quickly, who will pick you up and bring you home? Nobody.'" Annually, 300 to 470 people perish as they cross the Sonoran Desert into the United States.[17]

Missing from Juan Diego's list was that travel to the United States could also mean risking a marriage or other family ties. The omission made sense. If only barely, Juan Diego and Aurora's family had managed to survive despite migration's pleasures and dangers. But the two still needed to plot a way forward. Juan Diego wanted a new baby to place this phase in their marriage on the firmest footing he knew. Aurora balked at the idea and pressured Juan Diego to stop his drinking and the violent outbursts that went with it.

It was a bargain she was struggling to negotiate. Like other parts of her marriage, Aurora's choice of birth control was public knowledge. Aurora's aunt served as the village pharmacist and health promoter. One of Aurora's brothers once rattled off for me all the women he knew in Orozco and their preferred form of contraception. If Aurora went on birth control without her husband's consent, Juan Diego could accuse her of wanting to sleep with other men. Why else would she want consequence-free sex? The day I dropped by her house to talk, Aurora suspected she was already pregnant.

Other than the Evangelical churches and a few Alcoholics Anonymous groups in a neighboring town, the family had no recourse for dealing with Juan Diego's drinking. Like many Calakmuleños, Aurora and Juan Diego viewed problem drinking as a "vice," a shameful choice that Juan Diego made over and over again. Because so few people in Calakmul saw excessive alcohol consumption as a medical problem that could benefit from professional attention, I began to explain this idea to Aurora. I had heard in her voice feelings of guilt and recrimination, and I hoped to offer a perspective that let her know there might be something else going on here, something bigger than the two of them. "About the drinking," I began to say. Aurora cut me off, her girlish, giggly smile gone, her voice flat and matter-of-fact, her past pleasures replaced by present realities: "There's nothing good about it."

Notes

1. Hondagneu-Sotelo 1994: 66.
2. See also Hirsch 2003.
3. Padilla et al. 2007.
4. González-López 2005: 12.
5. McEvoy et al. 2012.
6. Hirsch et al. 2003.
7. Nilan and Feixa 2006.
8. Hirsch et al. 2009: 64.
9. González-López 2005.
10. Pitarch 2010: 75.
11. Boehm 2008; McEvoy et al. 2012; Rodman 2006.
12. Merry 1997.

13. Dreby 2009; Drotbohm 2010; Skolnik et al. 2012.
14. Hirsch et al. 2009: 65.
15. Maloka 1997.
16. Simmel 1950: 30.
17. Jimenez 2009. The U.S. Customs and Border Protection maintains official data on the number of border deaths: https://www.cbp.gov/newsroom/media-resources/stats. The Colibrí Center for Migrant Rights aids families who are searching for loved ones who disappear during a border crossing.

CHAPTER 6

Rosario: Coping with
a Husband's Return

Rosario did not choose her marriage partner—her mother-in-law, Elvia, arranged the relationship—but with her husband, Rafael, in the United States, Rosario enjoyed new freedoms. Living alone with her four daughters, she managed her house as she saw fit: "It is very different when Rafael is here. It's different because I know I have to get up early to cook for him, to make his breakfast. If a wife doesn't prepare her husband's breakfast, he won't leave home in a good mood. When he returns, I have to make sure his dinner is ready; then he will take his bath and have a rest." Unconstrained from her husband's schedule and flush with cash from his remittances, Rosario found a new pleasure in financial management. Rosario had always been energetic and a bit happy-go-lucky. Now, she turned that spirit to moneymaking and learned she had a special talent.

With the money Rafael sent, Rosario worked nearly every financial opportunity available to her. She opened a mom-and-pop grocery store and deposited a large sum with one of the county's shopkeepers who paid interest on the money they took in. She purchased land and built an investment house, which she planned to rent out as soon as it was completed. The building just needed a concrete floor and some kind of bathroom. She contributed to the "feminization of agriculture" that regularly follows men's labor migration by managing the family farm alongside all her other work.[1] Like most Ch'ol women, Rosario had always kept a flock of chickens and turkeys. Now she hired workers to plant, weed, and harvest five acres of cropland. She oversaw the sale of the family's cash crop. Rosario was not very interested in buying consumer goods. She saved and somehow invested even when Rafael was sporadic with his remittances. Her family and neighbors noticed Rosario's acumen and voiced their approval.

When her husband returned from the United States, Rosario saw her entrepreneurial activities come to an abrupt halt. After resuming his traditional position of household financial manager, Rafael chose to spend the family's money in a different way. There were few jobs available for Rafael in Zarajuato, and to cover expenses the family began to spend what they had saved during his trip abroad. Alarmingly for Rosario, Rafael chipped away at the financial foundation she laid down by binge drinking with his buddies. Prior to emigration, Rafael only occasionally drank to excess. Since his return, he was drinking regularly, and his alcohol consumption had become a serious problem.

Rafael now turned violent when he drank, and Rosario found herself on the receiving end of his aggressions. Fearing for her life, Rosario took to hiding the family's shotgun and machetes at any sign of a bender. She waited out the worst by hiding with her daughters in the family's cornfield or at her father's house. In Calakmul, women are not necessarily embarrassed into silence about battery the way they may be in the United States.[2] Rosario did not hide or downplay Rafael's violence. Instead, she spoke openly about it and pleaded with family and friends to encourage Rafael to change, "aconsejarlo."

Rosario had few options for dealing with the situation. Rafael ghosted about Zarajuato, a man stuck in a place where he did not belong. Return migrants enduring similar feelings of alienation often began to plan another trip to the United States. The pattern is common. Some researchers suggest emigrants' periods at home may be less about reincorporating themselves into their communities and more about getting a temporary reprieve from the strains of emigrant life.[3]

Rosario may have wished Rafael would travel abroad again, but she could not count on another round of emigration to free her from his abuse. Rafael had left the United States on the heels of the Great Recession. The recession began, in part, with the collapse of a real estate bubble, and the plentiful roofing jobs that had kept Rafael employed grew scarce. A steady trickle of migrants returning to Calakmul spread word that work was unavailable north of the border. Rafael felt trapped in Zarajuato, and Rosario felt trapped in her marriage.

In this chapter, we follow Rosario as she works to rid her marriage of multiple threats: her husband's infidelity, his alcoholism, and his physical violence toward her. When I asked the wives of emigrant men whether their husbands seemed changed when they returned, as often as not they replied, "He was the same, only he drank more." This suggested that their husbands also returned more aggressive. As in other places, violence in Calakmul was a common element of men's drunken behavior.[4]

As with the rate of migration-related divorces, it is impossible to know the precise effects of migration on men's problem drinking or other gendered stressors. The domestic violence that women such as Rosario and Aurora associated with their husbands' return also defied quantification. Nonetheless, I heard women's stories of men's infidelity, problem drinking, and domestic violence frequently enough that this chapter explores how these byproducts of migration might interact and reinforce one another. When Calakmuleño marriages and international migration grated against each other, the friction could start a conflagration.

Active stayers in Calakmul viewed the mix of migration-related alcohol consumption, infidelity, and intimate partner violence with some ambivalence. Calakmuleños took it for granted that migration easily led to substance abuse, just as they viewed men's travels as conducive to infidelity. They disparaged men like Rafael for allowing themselves to fall into migration's trap. Calakmuleños used the word *vicio*, or vice, to describe excessive alcohol and drug consumption, as well as sexual promiscuity. Vices, they said, arose from personal weakness. Men could choose to stop if they wished. It was disappointing and sad for the family involved, people said. But they believed that Rafael and migrants like him had run amok by taking the drinking and sex to an extreme. These men veered into the dangerous end of the pleasure-danger continuum and let themselves become "lost" in the "perversity" that abounds in the United States.[5]

At the same time, the prevalence of *vicio* among migrant men suggested to Calakmuleños there was something about international travel per se that encouraged bad behavior. Migration seemed to foster substance abuse and womanizing in men who showed no inclination toward these problems. Migration also seemed to exaggerate vices in men who already held these habits. Active stayers did not understand precisely the connection between migration and men's vices because they only had a rough understanding of men's lives north of the border. Thus, they came to view infidelity and problem drinking as personal choices that were *also* linked to men's travels.

In doing so, Calakmuleños drew a fuzzy boundary between migration's personal aspects and its invisible, distant qualities. They recognized that the friction inherent in international migration contained elements of "structural violence."[6] Paul Farmer, a proponent of eradicating structural violence, describes it as harm arising from "disparate access to resources, political power, education, health care, and legal standing."[7] Calakmuleños experienced structural violence when they became subject to government policies that devalued their crops and exposed them to international markets where they had few tools to compete. Because Calakmuleños had little influence over NAFTA and other state policies that undermined their livelihoods and encouraged their migration, these polices enacted structural violence. Calakmuleños were exposed to additional forms of structural violence including prejudice toward campesinos and Indigenous people, as well as the trauma of forced relocation. These harms arose from campesinos' lack of access to money, political power, and the other means to shape their life course.

Rosario's example highlights the way globalization's friction can also foster structural violence within people's intimate relationships. In previous chapters, we saw how men's migration placed women in impossible situations as they broke gender norms in order to achieve a family's financial goals. We also saw how men's labor migration created vulnerabilities to sexual infidelity for both partners. Rosario's example shows migration could forge a chain of aggressions stretching from US construction sites to Calakmuleños' own homes. The result for some women was real, face-to-face hostility, which Rosario barely managed to survive.[8]

Although men's infidelity, alcohol abuse, and violence interacted to women's detriment, Calakmuleños did not treat the three activities the same. Whereas they readily gossiped about men's drinking and womanizing, the larger rumor network fell conspicuously quiet when it came to domestic violence. The lack of talk was noticeable, because women like Rosario regularly sought to use public opinion to pressure their husbands to change (Figure 6.1). Migration-related intimate violence received little public attention because, as we saw with Aurora, wives were not expected to have enjoyable lives. To the contrary, wives were expected to tolerate their husbands' tempers. Domestic violence could be bound up with alcohol consumption and infidelity as normal expressions of men's prerogatives and as the normal suffering women were expected to undergo in their marriages.[9]

Certainly not all men engaged in battery,[10] but for those who did, Calakmuleños recognized there were legitimate and illegitimate acts of intimate partner abuse. Prior to international migration, when marriages were built on shared farming, violent men might cite their wives' laziness

FIGURE 6.1
Along with patrilocal residence, multi-generational families are common in Calakmul, which allows senior women to monitor family behavior either directly or through gossip networks. This picture shows three generations of a single family.
Photo: Luis Melodelgado

or poor housekeeping as excuses for their behavior.[11] A man's violence gained the veneer of acceptability if he could demonstrate his wife failed to carry her share of the workload. A man crossed the line into unacceptable behavior if his wife was clearly without fault. For example, Calakmuleños frowned upon young men who beat their wives in the earliest years of a marriage. Because young men initiated marriages, and a young wife was considered to be in the process of learning her duties, it seemed wrong that a young man should find fault with his new partner. Drunken battery was also considered unacceptable, as the violence clearly arose from the man's inebriation and not from any action on the wife's part.

Still, even in cases of unacceptable battery, Calakmuleños hesitated to intervene in what they considered to be other people's troubles. These dynamics left women like Rosario with scant resources to confront problematic behavior now exacerbated by international migration. Interestingly, Rosario's repertoire had some tools to address Rafael's infidelity, since the larger Calakmul society was invested in keeping married couples together. But Calakmuleños were less invested in men's sobriety and equanimity. To the contrary, Calakmuleños expected men to have the upper hand over women.

These beliefs limited women like Rosario in their ability to defend themselves against a danger migration posed that was unique to them. International migration can intensify domestic violence by frustrating men's ability to enact their version of masculinity and by fostering additional, acute stressors within men's lives. For women, the same domestic violence can reduce their options and weaken what energies women do have to act in self-defense.[12]

As we shall see, in Rosario's case, when her existing repertoire failed to protect her from her husband, she saved her life by invoking the new gender norms Calakmuleños had crafted in response to migration. In doing so, she also saved her marriage.

It is important to note at the outset that, as in many cases of intimate partner violence, this outcome was by no means assured. In addition to her limited resources, Rosario was working with a problem whose roots in globalization were only partly visible to her. The people and forces fostering a violent migration lay outside her influence. Nonetheless, Rosario managed to exercise constrained choice despite the odds. And her example offers a larger lesson that reveals migration to be driven partly by localized gender norms, partly by the impersonal demands migration imposed, and partly by personal decision making.

Rescuing a Marriage on the Brink

For Rosario, Rafael's drinking and violence were especially vexing, since few wives worked harder than she did to rescue her marriage from crisis and secure her husband's return. While in the United States, Rafael carried out an affair that left Rosario and her four daughters at risk of abandonment. The fallout from the affair also jeopardized Rafael's health, which Rosario took upon herself to remedy.

Rosario knew little of Rafael's paramour until the relationship had developed into a second marriage. Rafael had always viewed migration as an escape from family life, and after his arranged marriage he had good reason to strike out on his own. On his second trip to Alabama, Rafael seized the chance to start life over. Rosario had been opposed to this journey and tried to dissuade Rafael from traveling. But Rafael's brother Jacobo lured him with promises of jobs earning $9.50 an hour. Upon returning to the United States, Rafael became reacquainted with a woman he had met during his first trip. The two fell in love and began to live together. Rafael told me he considered himself *juntado*, or "joined" to this woman. *Juntado* is a word Calakmuleños use to describe relationships they recognize as marriages, although the couple has not had a legal or religious ceremony. By choosing this word, Rafael was indicating that he considered his new relationship as enduring as any marriage could be.

Like nearly all Calakmuleño men who engaged in stateside affairs, Rafael kept his new partner a secret from his wife. He planned to fulfill his responsibilities to Rosario by continuing his financial support. Rafael also kept Rosario and their children a secret from his new partner. The relationship became public after the new wife discovered a photograph of Rosario in Rafael's wallet. The woman chose to end the relationship, and in the turmoil that followed, Rafael became racked by a four-month headache that occasionally affected his eyesight. He got drunk every day. He could not seem to stop crying, and he could not get a good night's sleep. His brother Jacobo finally telephoned Rosario for help. The calls flew back and forth as family on both sides of the border fretted over Rafael's situation and whether he could be cured.

It was Rosario's resourcefulness that brought Rafael back to health. Rosario traveled two hours to visit a faith healer, Samuel, whom Elvia and other family members had sometimes consulted for their own medical needs. Rosario is a devout Christian and for her, as for her family and neighbors, the Bible is the word of God. Indeed, Rosario's father is a Pentecostal preacher. These beliefs, however, did not dampen her interest in the magical arts. Like most Christians, Rosario ascribed to a localized faith that regarded the Bible and church teachings as compatible with her cultural viewpoints. Among these viewpoints, Rosario and other Calakmuleños took for granted that people are connected to one another through a hidden dimension, one that is unaffected by long distances. Healers like Samuel had special powers to access this realm. Calakmul's healers, in turn, positioned their work within Christian frameworks by crediting their skills to God's will. As Samuel explained, he might have access to commanding spirits but without God's will, saints and spirits were powerless to intervene in human affairs.

Thinking Rosario might not be the only wife to seek out Samuel's help, I met with the healer to ask him about his work. Samuel managed to communicate both mystery and authority upon first sight. A man in his early sixties, Samuel had salt-and-pepper hair and the upright posture of someone poised to voice an opinion. The thatch-and-pole structure he built to receive patients gave off a clinical air that conveyed medical expertise. Samuel had added to the one-room building a covered porch with a row of three chairs, reminiscent of a doctor's waiting room. Inside, Samuel had fashioned a kind of examining table. Samuel told me he did not like publicity, because many people associated healers with the dark arts. To avoid unwelcome scrutiny, he located his clinic inside a patch of woods and had hung tarps on the building's walls to obscure the interior.

Samuel described men like Rafael as having an ailment that he believed commonly afflicted migrants in the United States. Samuel drew this conclusion from information he gleaned from spirit guides and a mystical *pantalla* or "screen" that worked something like a television. The guides and screen allowed Samuel to observe far-away events. Samuel had never traveled to the United States, but his sources led him to understand that migrant men became tied to their stateside paramours in ways the men could not see. Migrant men may have surrounded their affairs with secrecy, but their mistresses had their own surreptitious powers.

Women in the United States, Samuel said, used the services of a healer to sew a "thread" within the man. The thread tied the man to his mistress such that if he returned to Mexico, the lover could pull him back north of the border. A jealous woman could also use the thread to leave a man impotent, so if he did manage to stay with his wife, he could no longer have sexual relations with her. In Samuel's words:

> What happens there in the United States is that they [the lover and her
> sorcerer] kill the husband's member. Why do people do this? Out of

spite. They see the man is thinking of returning to Mexico, and so they cause him harm. They do not want the man to be happy here. Then, the wife comes to me to ask for help.

What happens is that people in the United States do not think people here can help these sick men. They think nobody is going to see the thread, and that they have stronger powers. What they do not know is that we healers are like karate fighters. Some have yellow belts, and some have brown and black belts. Here in Mexico, we healers work with God, with the Living Spirit. Whose power could be greater than his?

Rafael's paramour had forced the separation, so this diagnosis did not exactly fit his case. Nonetheless, Samuel told Rosario that Rafael suffered from an imperceptible enchantment. Samuel would sever the tie that bound Rafael to the United States, but he also needed Rosario's help. Following Samuel's instructions, Rosario shipped a particular kind of vitamin to Alabama to help Rafael recoup any lost strength.

Samuel expressed in poetic terms Calakmuleños' reservations toward men leaving their families despite the economic reward. As a metaphor for migration's hidden workings, Samuel suggested that part of the structural violence of migration entailed robbing the region of men and their virility. Migration placed men's virility at the service of formidable foreign women, some of whom used their powers to neuter. This redirection of men's energies could render Calakmuleños unable to reproduce their society whether a migrant man returned home or not. By cleansing a migrant of foreign sex, Samuel removed the violence of migration-induced adultery, reestablished a man's sexual connection to his wife, and made possible social regeneration more generally.

Listening to Samuel as he talked about working on behalf of wives, I noticed that his beliefs were firmly rooted in Calakmul's patriarchal norms. Overall, he blamed women for men's problems. As a solution to migration's ills, he prescribed repositioning men as the fertile, authoritative heads of their households.

And in that regard, Rosario's efforts worked. Immediately after her first visit to Samuel, she telephoned Rafael the diagnosis. About a week later, Rafael's headaches cleared up. The vitamins Rosario shipped to Alabama restored Rafael to full health. All this took place in 2007 and 2008, just before the Great Recession. With the collapse of the US real estate bubble, roofing jobs dried up. Rafael lingered in Alabama as long as he could financially endure before heading back to Zarajuato. However, rather than credit the declining US economy with his homecoming, Rafael thanked Rosario and Samuel for bringing him back. Without them, he said, he would have remained in the United States forever.

By turning to a faith healer, Rosario found in her repertoire a way to address her husband's infidelity, but the same formula would not work for his drinking and the violence that came with it. It is relevant that Rafael sought relief from the demise of his US marriage by turning to the bottle. It is also relevant that Samuel did not see Rafael's drinking as part of the larger problem.

Instead, Samuel acted selectively on the situation, focusing on an adultery that offended him because it placed men in inferior positions toward women. Samuel made sense of this gender subversion by ascribing it to far-away, female culprits and their witchcraft. In comparison, drinking offered no identifiable villain other than a man's own predilection, and Samuel's support of men's authority kept him from curtailing a man's freedom to drink. Rosario would have to find help elsewhere to counteract Rafael's alcohol consumption—a difficult proposition, given how international migration added to long-standing social structures that fueled men's substance abuse.

Alcohol-Infused Migration

When Rosario and other women remarked that their emigrant husbands returned home "the same" but "drank more," they pointed to the way international migration added a new twist to the long-lasting role of alcohol abuse in their lives. Despite Calakmuleños' notions of alcohol consumption as a vice that men chose, alcoholism is also part of a structural violence that has been inflicted on Mexico's poor for centuries.[13] In order to understand migration-related drinking as women lived the problem—and why women encountered little support to stop men's drinking—it is helpful to understand how migration both built on this history of alcohol abuse and altered the structures that encouraged men's drinking. Alcohol consumption is cultural. People drink in particular settings, with particular people, in order to cultivate particular kinds of feelings that connect them with some people but not others. People's personal decisions surrounding drinking take place within larger social structures.[14] In Mexico, alcohol has played a central role in governance, which meant that for Calakmuleños, liquor held multiple and compelling associations with power.

The tools Rosario used to stop Rafael's drinking—alternately increasing public and family pressure and retreating into a resentful silence—have been well-honed by generations of Mexican women. Rural women especially developed these tools because they lived in places where alcohol consumption was integral to creating and maintaining social hierarchies. During the 1800s and early 1900s, state authorities across Mexico relied on alcohol taxes for most of their revenue.[15] This was just one way elites used alcohol to channel money from the poorest parts of Mexican society to the wealthiest.

Another way entailed using alcohol to create a virtually captive group of laborers. This was the experience of Rosario's and Rafael's great-grandparents who, in the early twentieth century, worked on coffee plantations owned by US investors (see Chapter 3). The plantations' managers foisted alcohol onto workers in order to put them in debt to the estates.[16] The debts accompanied slave-like conditions and were so important to the estates' operations that one estate manager admitted that coffee plantations ran on liquor like "an automobile runs on gas."[17] (When US employers occasionally pay wages in alcohol, turn a blind eye to drinking on the job, or reward crews with a round of beers at the end of the day, they echo this exploitative use of alcohol. Anthropologist Jason Pine views the problem of work and intoxicants as requiring further study. He argues that capitalism seems to demand an intoxicated body capable of adapting to market logics: "From Starbucks to energy drinks, steroids to Viagra, and Prozac to Provigil . . . workplace and everyday doping have become normalized, expected, and in some cases even mandatory.")[18]

Historically, Mexicans, almost always male Mexicans, have also used liquor to climb the social ladder and advertise their high social standing. I saw this first-hand in Calakmul in the early 1990s, when I watched local elites show off their wealth by drinking and carousing. Campesino leaders mingled in cantinas, where they partied with cantina waitresses. After a few hours at the bar, the inebriated men ventured out to a dance or other public place with a waitress on their arm. These performances spoke to a cultural definition of power as an "intimate and gendered world suffused with all sorts of prohibited desires."[19]

When Calakmuleños began to migrate, they carried with them an understanding of alcohol consumption as indicative of power and powerlessness alike. One way to think about migration-related drinking would be to consider whether men don't see in their stateside boozing the chance to flip their status from a person who drinks because he is poor to that of a person who drinks because he is rich. Regardless of the answer to this question, once in the United States, migrant men encountered forces—hidden from women like Rosario—that encouraged their drinking in new ways. This aspect of men's migration was not universal. Some undocumented men report that intense work schedules and the need to be on guard at all times from immigration authorities forces them into sobriety. These men tend to drink less than their visa-holding counterparts do at the same job sites.[20]

Nonetheless, in his case, Rafael was subject to a series of risk factors known to increase migrant men's odds of substance abuse. Some of the risks were intrinsic to men's labor migration and accumulated atop any lingering effects of the perilous border crossing.[21] The risks Rafael underwent included

- Living without the support of female family members or senior men
- Hearing bad news from home and feeling shame at an inability to solve the problems
- Moving about in social isolation from the dominant society
- Enduring years of anxiety as a result of being undocumented
- Encountering new forms of prejudice and discrimination
- Living in a rural area with few entertainment outlets
- Performing sixty hours or more of intense physical labor every week
- Feeling peer pressure to drink from relatives and neighbors suffering the same stressors

Another aspect of migration also affected men's drinking. Researchers find the longer a migrant man stays in the United States, the more likely he is to have substance abuse problems because of migration-related trauma he undergoes *inside* the United States.[22] This temporal structure was another hidden aspect of men's labor migration, and it impacted Calakmuleños with greater force than it had past generations of Mexican migrants.

Calakmuleños like Rafael joined the migration stream at a particular moment in history; they did so just when travelers were planning longer stays to compensate for an increasingly expensive and life-threatening border crossing. The 1990s saw smugglers charge a five-fold increase for their services in real terms.[23] The rising costs were the result of a cat and mouse game between US border patrol and smugglers. Beginning in 1992, the United States increased the number of border patrol agents and the equipment at their disposal. Smugglers responded by finding new and dangerous routes into the United States and passing the extra costs on to migrants.[24] Smugglers' fees around the time of Rafael's first trip in 2001 were roughly $1,300; when he traveled again in 2006, he paid $3,500. (As of writing, the costs can range between $7-10,000.) Rafael's first trip to the United States lasted fourteen months. His second trip stretched out to four years with an accompanying increase in his risk of substance abuse.[25]

The stressors that encouraged Rafael's problem drinking continued after he returned home, when Rosario became directly exposed to their consequences. While he was away, Rafael provided amply for his wife and children. Upon return, Rafael had to rebuild his place in the family while adjusting to a labor market that offered sporadic employment, low pay, and doubts about his manhood. "In the United States, you work and at the end of the day, you have some money to buy food and clothes," Rafael told me. "Here you work one whole day and you can't afford anything. And sometimes, they don't pay you." A Mexican proverb observes: *Quien no tranza, no avanza*; he who doesn't cheat, doesn't advance. Being paid less for a day's work in Mexico than he earned in one hour in the United States, Rafael naturally felt cheated.

Having been rewarded as a hard worker in Alabama, Rafael was taken aback when friends and neighbors now questioned his abilities. Calakmuleños described work in the United States as "soft," easy in comparison to farming by machete. Migrant men were considered "soft" by association, and when they returned home they had to reestablish their credentials as laborers. Because migrant men temporarily ceased to participate in locally recognizable forms of masculinity, upon their return they found themselves feminized in the eyes of the larger Calakmul society.[26]

All of this had an effect on intimate partner violence in migrant households. Differences over "who should earn how much by doing what kind of work, where and with whom; how and when money should be spent on what" can become core issues of marital conflict and arenas where men attempt to reassert their authority through domestic violence.[27] Rafael responded to the repeated economic dislocation that migration gave rise to in his life by drinking too much, and the drinking led to his becoming abusive.

For women like Rosario, the violence was yet another assertion that migration's pleasures and dangers were gendered. In Calakmul, women like Rosario might join in the drinking from the privacy of their homes, but for the most part wives were assigned the role Rosario acquired, that of "designated driver." Rosario and other women tended to men who were in a drunken state or sick with hangovers. They kept their families together while alcohol meted out its destruction. Researchers of problem drinking show that for people living a life of ceaseless hardship, binge drinking can offer moments of joy. Through alcohol, people can create moments that are "musical, romantic, salacious, death-accepting, and much given to the . . . staging of hilarious events."[28] In the midst of migration's many aggressions, the pleasures of these momentary reprieves were less available to the wives of emigrant men. In their marriages, women were expected to manage the dangers of an alcohol-infused migration regardless of the consequences to their personal well-being.

The Intimate Violence of Migration

Rosario knew little of the structural violence that encouraged her husband's intimate aggressions. It is possible that had she known about the roots of his behavior, these causes would seem unimportant to her. In moments of crisis, Rosario needed to protect her life. During Rafael's emigration, Rosario trained her formidable energies on the family's finances and then on securing her husband's return. During the time of Rafael's boozing and violence, she marshaled her vigor and liveliness to her own self-defense.

The protective mechanisms available to Rosario included

- Seeking solace with family and friends
- Commiserating with women in similar situations
- Finding ways to handle particularly problematic behavior
- Securing help from extended kin to deal with an abusive husband
- Growing older and, therefore, independent of her husband; older women were also believed to draw strength from their accumulated experiences
- Converting to a religion that promoted abstinence and whose worshippers understood the challenges a wife endured

Rural Zarajuato had no domestic violence shelter and no resident police force to intervene in domestic disputes. In the early twenty-first century, state health officials opened a domestic violence hotline, but Zarajuato's only telephone was located blocks away from Rosario's house in one of the town's mom-and-pop shops. Given that the people answering the hotline lived in a distant city, it was unclear how Rosario and other women might use the service to get help during a violent episode. All in all, the protective measures available to Rosario offered a possible escape from her husband's immediate threat. Rosario had no means to change the social forces that put her in the way of intimate violence. Thankfully, for Rosario the temporary escapes were successful escapes.

With her characteristic verve, Rosario worked the angles available to her. When I spoke with Rosario and Rafael together, Rosario sat silently, assuming the role of the second-in-command wife but visibly seething at her husband's excuses. Rafael said that, despite recurring alcohol-induced blackouts, his problem was not out of control. He was drinking less than he had in the past, since he was no longer drinking daily. Rosario would only respond with a sardonic "*¿Ya ves?*" "You see what I have to deal with?" Meanwhile, she found excuses to spend as much time as possible in the company of her sisters and female neighbors, some of whom were encountering similar problems with their husbands. The women cooked meals together, visited during their free time, and sent news of their daily activities via their children, who roamed between houses. In these settings, Rosario readily reported Rafael's latest drinking bout or hangover. She stoked the rumor mill to pressure Rafael to change.

Rosario's most effective tactic involved fulfilling cultural ideals of the hardworking wife. By carrying out her household and farming duties, Rosario took the moral high ground and shored up her status as an honorable woman worthy of a hardworking, supportive partner. She demonstrated that she was holding up her end of the marital bargain, and she lavished public praise on Rafael when he did the same. At one point, the couple feared the shopkeeper with whom Rosario had deposited money might refuse to return their cash, a common occurrence in this underground banking system. Rosario's sister and brother-in-law had to make repeated requests to recover the $6,000 they had invested with the grocer. Rafael showed up at the grocer's with suitcases in hand, announcing that he was leaving the country and he needed his money immediately. Maybe the grocer was moved by Rafael's faked need, or maybe he just happened to have cash at the ready. Whatever the case, the trick worked, and Rosario crowed at Rafael's cleverness.

While elsewhere in Calakmul migration was changing marital bargains to emphasize consumerism and personal fulfillment, Rosario's adherence to older marital ideals may have buoyed her during this time in her life. The anthropologist Laura McClusky (2001) argues that repertoires that include marriages built on complementary work roles can help women maintain self-regard should they experience domestic abuse. For Rosario, her family, and her neighbors, a woman's responsibilities in her marriage were clearly defined. Menaced as she was, Rosario knew that as long as she fulfilled those responsibilities, her larger social standing was secure and she should feel no shame at her husband's behavior.

One by one, over Rosario's protests, Rafael cashed out her investments in order to support his drinking habit. Meanwhile, Rosario fought to protect her most valuable asset of all: the rental house. Rosario continued to hope she could complete the construction and find a tenant who could provide the family with a monthly income. In my mind, the house stood as a symbol of the uncertain ability of international migration to empower women. Prior to emigration, women did not have houses of their own. They lived in their father's or husband's house. But everyone called the investment "Rosario's." The property's legal title was in her name. Yet like her partially completed house, Rosario's empowerment depended on a continued flow of US dollars. Upon his return, Rafael presumed he could dispose of the house as he wished.

Rosario reacted by refusing to tell Rafael exactly where the house was located. Extended family members were reluctant to put themselves in the middle of a marital dispute, so they also refused to tell him. Rafael did eventually learn the house's location from Calakmul's gossip network, although Rosario managed to use her ownership to forestall any sale.

Meanwhile Rafael's drinking continued, until an exhausted Rosario announced she would divorce him if he did not stop. Her resolve was unshakable. If Calakmul had not been drawn into international migration streams, Rosario would probably not have viewed divorce as an option. In general, a woman's economic vulnerability can keep her trapped in an abusive relationship. Yet migration had forced Rosario to rely on her own resources, first when her husband was away, and again when he returned.

Rosario saw that she could live without Rafael and, just maybe, thrive in his absence. When she threatened to end the marriage, she did so with a conviction that forced Rafael to take notice.[29]

Faced with the unbearable prospect of living alone, Rafael conceded. He agreed to cooperate with Rosario in exploring a sobriety that would work for both of them. Together, the couple pieced together information distributed by a local health clinic on the effects of problem drinking. They took inspiration from relatives, including both their fathers, who had stopped drinking by joining an Evangelical church. With their more modest faith, the couple balked at the expressions of religious fervor often linked to conversion. Instead, they drew on Rafael's time in Alabama, where he learned about a more secular path to sobriety. After being stopped for a DUI, Rafael received a sentence requiring he attend Alcoholics Anonymous meetings. Rafael did not adopt cultural ideas of alcoholism prevalent in the United States. In the United States, "addiction" tends to refer to a "chronic disease," and sufferers are expected to choose recovery from an illness that, paradoxically, has been defined as a lifelong affliction.[30] *Rafael continued to view his behavior as a vice within his control. Nonetheless, the AA meetings planted a seed. Finally, Rafael did stop drinking altogether, to the extent that, in subsequent years, he recalled his earlier drinking bouts with sheepish embarrassment.*

Rafael's sobriety allowed the couple to realize a shared entrepreneurial vision that could take advantage of Rosario's financial skills. They reopened the mom-and-pop shop and cooperated in its management. They planned their family's financial future together.

When I visited the couple in 2015, they said that now that they understood the endeavor more fully, they both wanted another try at Rafael's emigration. This time they felt prepared to meet its challenges, and barring the unexpected—another illness, an accident at work, a deportation—they were confident they could use migration to secure their dream for their family. Rosario was confident Rafael would work as hard as ever and, in the United States, his efforts would be rewarded. Rafael felt equally sure Rosario would manage the money well. Rosario would use the remittances to buy a piece of land next to a busy road—a perfect site for a shop. Since grocery stores abound in Zarajuato, the couple planned to offer clothing and maybe hardware items. The last time I saw Rosario

*and Rafael, they were raising money for the trip and keeping an
ear to the ground to assess whether opportunity had returned to
the US job market.*

Notes

1. Deere 2005.
2. See McClusky 2001.
3. Striffler (2007) makes this assertion in regards to migrants' brief, holiday visits to Mexico. I extend this argument to the longer stays men regularly undertake in a life of circular migration.
4. On the association between alcohol and domestic violence, see Eber 1995; McClusky 2001; Merry 2000. For comparison, it is noteworthy that overall Mexicans are less likely to drink alcohol than their neighbors to the north. National data also shows US residents are more likely than Mexicans to smoke marijuana and consume cocaine (Borges et al. 2011; Degenhardt et al. 2008). A key difference between the two countries is the way alcohol has functioned in particular contexts (Mitchell 2004).
5. See also Duke and Gómez Carpinterio 2009.
6. Holmes 2013; Vogt 2013.
7. Farmer et al. 2006: 449.
8. This chapter focuses on domestic violence in the form of beatings, but the aggressions women suffered likely went further. As Brettell notes in her 2017 review of marriage and migration across the world, migration has been associated with heightened marital rape, the manipulation of reproductive rights, and where the practice is part of the local cultural repertoire, bride burning. Mexicans are not the only people on the planet who see American sexual norms as libertine, and this fact also impacts incidence of marital rape. Reviewing the research on Indian emigration to the United States, Brettell notes that sexual violence within marriages "is further exacerbated by a perception of American society as sexually permissive and the desire of South Asian men to have as much control as they can over their wives' sexuality (2017: 89)."
9. See Adelman 2017; Menjívar 2011.
10. Gutmann 1997.
11. McClusky 2001.
12. Adelman 2017.
13. Mitchell 2004.
14. Because much of the research on alcohol and, by extension, drug abuse focuses on poor people, and poor people of color at that, Crawford's 2019

book on *Dealing with Privilege* is compelling. Crawford describes how whiteness and middle-class standing both structure suburban drug dealing in particular ways and protect dealers themselves from the drugs' negative consequences. Work like that of Crawford's illuminates migration-related substance abuse by clarifying the way social structures intersect with people's drug and alcohol consumption to foster diverse outcomes.

15. Carey 2014.
16. Bobrow-Strain 2007.
17. Bunzel in Eber 1995: 30.
18. Pine 2007: 363. See also García 2008; Worby and Organista 2007. Historically in the United States, employers also paid workers in alcohol to create submissive populations. This was the case with textile mills in the Southeast, and I thank Carol Ann Lewald for pointing out this connection. Over the course of the twentieth century, drinking on the job grew less acceptable in the United States because work in both the office and in the factory increasingly required a precision that was undermined by drugs that dulled the senses. As Pine (2007) notes, the drugs that facilitate work now tend to include coffee as well as methamphetamines, cocaine, and prescription drugs such as Aderall. In general, when it comes to workplace doping, alcohol, heroin and other painkillers are more favored by blue-collar workers whose jobs place wear-and-tear on the body. Cocaine and Aderall are more likely to be favored by office workers who seek to increase their productivity and who associate these drugs with middle-class status (Crawford 2019).
19. DeVries 2002: 904.
20. Garcini et al. 2017.
21. García 2008.
22. Worby and Organista 2007.
23. Cornelius 2001.
24. Donato et al. 2006.
25. Between 1992 and 2009, the number of US border patrol staff rose from 3,555 to 17,415 agents (costs to taxpayers rose from $3.26 million to $2.7 billion, see Hinojosa-Ojeda 2012). Smugglers increased their fees accordingly. This stepwise dynamic is important because in order to recoup the cost of the crossing, migrants stay longer in the United States. The longer a migrant stays in the United States the less likely he or she is to return (Fernández-Kelly and Massey 2007). The role that increasing border security plays in expanding the undocumented population in the United States has been known to researchers for two decades. But the information is entirely ignored in US debates about border security.

26. For more on how men's migration can feminize them in the eyes of their home communities, see Brettell 2017.
27. Adelman 2017: 164.
28. Mitchell 2004: 32.
29. Two more innovations were crucial to allowing women like Rosario to manage without a husband. The first was the opening in Calakmul of a government office where women could sue men for child support. The second was a welfare program, then known as Oportunidades, that supports women and children. In a 2010 survey, my colleagues and I asked 455 people (half men, half women) questions that probed the role of Oportunidades in decision making surrounding migration. Of the respondents, 77 percent agreed with the statement: "Some families rely on Oportunidades to survive the first months of a man's migration," when men typically have yet to earn surplus income sufficient to remit. Men and women agreed with this statement in roughly equal proportions. In response to a second statement, "Some men who migrate send less money because they know their wives receive Oportunidades" 61 percent of women agreed and 46 percent of men agreed. In this way, state welfare offered women like Rosario sufficient income to imagine life without an abusive husband while it also subsidized men's travels. The program also required that women attend health care talks, where domestic violence was a regular topic of conversation. While these talks could also create a backlash against women (see Schmook et al. 2018), with Rosario they encouraged her to think differently about her husband's behavior.
30. Garcia 2010: 15.

CHAPTER 7

....

Berta: Healing Families

Shifting to get comfortable in her white plastic folding chair, Berta nearly dropped the unwieldy stack of notebooks in her hands. A seventy-three-year-old great-grandmother, Berta wore a simple, rectangular shift with a flowered print of black and white. She had welcomed me into her home, where she received all her clients, presuming I was another admirer of her healing prowess. The efficacy of Berta's magical prayers, midwifery, and herbal medicines had been chronicled by Calakmul's local newspaper and radio station, as well as by the county's extensive rumor mill. Her renown was such that the taxi driver who dropped me off knew who she was and where she lived even though he had never been to her house. Berta knew she was famous and, during our conversation, recited a catalog of the distant communities from where women and men had traveled in search of her services. Berta tended to speak in lists. As for the strange foreigner who had arrived on her doorstep, Berta saw me as another in a line of complimentary interviewers.

I sought out Berta after hearing the wives and mothers of emigrant men speak about her. Some of the women had turned to Berta to heal family disputes. Others told me they were skeptical of the value of her work. They suspected Berta was herself a party to their migration-related suffering. In Mexico, "curanderos" or healers are often accused of using their skills to inflict harm. Some women alleged Berta had added to migration's dangers by bewitching them and making them sick on behalf of a jealous neighbor or family member.

Speaking in a forceful Spanish inflected with the staccato rhythms of her native language, Yucatecan Maya, Berta explained how she used the notebooks. Each page included the name of one or two people for whom she prayed. Through her prayers, Berta wielded what she called her "power." Sometimes her prayers worked by entering the body of the person she prayed for. Other times her words acted by cutting through the cacophony of entreaties people regularly directed to the saints and spirits and to God. In either case, Berta told me, words she herself uttered stood a greater chance of producing the desired result than the petitions of the average person.

The notebooks helped Berta keep track of all the people she prayed for. Alongside the person's name, Berta jotted down the person's home village. If someone was living in the United States, she noted the name of that person's residence in Mexico. Berta worked from one notebook at a time, so the collection of five she showed me was an archival record of all the people she had treated in the past few years.

Often Berta's clients asked her to pray for someone else. A mother might ask Berta to pray for a son in the United States or for a daughter-in-law in Mexico. A young wife might ask Berta to pray for her husband or her mother-in-law. Clients asked Berta to use her powers to change their relatives. Berta didn't just heal individual bodies. From her perspective, she countered migration's dangers by healing relationships. In these cases, Berta wrote in her notebook the name of the target of such prayers as well as the supplicant on whose behalf she sent entreaties.

Migrant families brought all sorts of concerns to Berta, making her inventory of requests quite lengthy. Berta understood that the climate and weather in the United States were different from those in Calakmul, and travelers unaccustomed to these conditions could become ill. Berta prayed to cure men's illnesses. Unsurprisingly, family members were also concerned about men's vices. Berta understood that men who traveled to the United States may turn to drink or drugs, because "they're free to do so;

it's their lives. They're far from their families." Berta prayed for these men to turn their thoughts to God. A man's freedom could cause him to acquire a new mode of living and new habits. As a result, he might forget his family. If a man stopped telephoning, the reason was likely to be that he had forgotten his family. Berta prayed for these men to remember their families. Another indication that a man had stopped thinking about his family was that he ceased sending money home. Berta prayed for men to send money. She also prayed on behalf of family members who received money but wanted their relative to send more.

Berta prayed for Calakmul's active stayers as well. Mothers-in-law, she said, sought her services "because their daughters-in-law are dating other men." Choosing language a mother might use to scold an unruly child, Berta said she prayed to "aplacar la nuera," to get the daughter-in-law to "settle down."

Migration frequently created envidia *or "envy" among family and neighbors, according to Berta. This envy was simultaneously an emotion and an illness. Jealous people, Calakmuleños believed, could use sorcery to cause the recipient of their dissatisfaction to become sick. Calakmuleños called the resulting illness "envy." As Berta understood it, "people without family in the North have nothing. They have no money; they're simply poor. They farm their fields, and maybe they have money around the time they harvest. But people with family in the North receive money every week, every two weeks, or every month." Her eyes lit up, "And it's good money." (Berta herself occasionally received money from a young man in the United States on whose behalf she prayed.) Envy stood out as the most common complaint her clients brought her, but Berta tended to all sorts of hard feelings caused by newfound wealth.*

For the right price, Berta would minister to nearly any problem. One woman I knew was convinced Berta had healed her son of envy-induced diarrhea, a condition supposedly brought on by the woman's mother-in-law. Because children are not yet fully formed, people in Calakmul consider them more susceptible to witchcraft than adults. Daughter-in-law and mother-in-law had tussled for years over remittances, and with Berta's help the younger woman identified the source of her son's ailment in these arguments. "She wants the money!" the woman exclaimed of her mother-in-law. A healthy baby was priceless, but as a financial manager, the daughter-in-law couldn't help but report Berta's fee with raised eyebrows: Berta had charged her the equivalent of nearly two months' earnings for the average Calakmuleño.

There was, however, one important exception to the tasks Berta was willing to undertake. As a mother-in-law herself, when a daughter-in-law sought Berta's help, she often took the side of the older generation in the dispute. She did so quietly, without alerting the daughter-in-law to her actions. Berta had her own ideas of family order she wanted to enact. And because Berta's healing operated within a hidden realm invisible to the casual observer, the young woman had no way of knowing exactly what Berta was up to.

Because of their belief in the magic of healers, when Calakmuleños began to travel internationally, their journeys were different from those of travelers who do not share such beliefs. Wherever magic is practiced and receives broad social support, "it does indeed work."[1] By tapping into a healer's powers, Calakmuleños believed they could connect through a hidden dimension and across long distances. With the healer's help, a person might influence another's thoughts and emotional life. Healers, people said, could contribute to migration's dangers by sowing arguments that caused people to become estranged. Healers could also give life to migration's pleasures by causing people to fall in love or revive a love that had dimmed with distance.

In this chapter, we learn how Calakmuleños turned to healers like Berta to alleviate both the physical and emotional separations caused by migration. In the face of a globalized migration, healers like Berta enabled Calakmuleños to fashion a kind of magical localism. The social forces propelling migration were largely outside Calakmuleños' purview. Women were at a particular disadvantage when it came to seeing men's stateside lives. Yet Calakmuleños' own hidden dimension, the Otherworldly sphere in which healers moved, was a place they could turn to make sense of migration, ameliorate its hazards, and mend the family bonds migration left in tatters.

The type of healing Berta offered long pre-dated migration. Thus, Calakmuleños turned to the Otherworldly because it was a site where they were already accustomed to working through interpersonal matters. If anything, the novelty migration brought to healing was that people could now afford curanderos and use their services to address migration-related problems. Migration created conflict by forcing travelers and active stayers to tap into diverse parts of their repertoire or acquire altogether new beliefs and new practices.[2] But Calakmuleños mainly saw men and women behaving (or misbehaving) as husbands, wives, and mothers-in-law. In using the Otherworldly to influence one another's migration-related behavior or explain why a family member made disturbing migration-related decisions, Calakmuleños were, again, emphasizing the personal quality of a globalized migration.

As the active stayers who bore the brunt of migration's impacts, women constituted the larger portion of healers' clients. By turning to healers to address relationships gone awry, women acted out of self-preservation, out of concern for their loved ones, but also out of fear of one culture change in particular.

Arguments between in-laws and migration-related divorce were evidence that men's departures could sever family ties completely. In all times and in all places, families are foundational to how people carry out their lives. As Elvia taught me (see chapter 1), for Calakmuleños, marriage served as the cornerstone of family life. Married couples sat at the center of a constellation of people who took part in the ebb and flow of each other's daily lives. Migration's effects on marriage raised doubts about how—and whether—Calakmuleños might create new families in the future. Would life as they knew it survive migration?

Healers could not dispel these doubts. Nor could they guarantee their efforts would bring harmony to family relationships. Calakmuleños knew, and their healers emphasized, that in the larger picture all people were at the mercy of God's will. God's intentions were, by definition, unfathomable. With this caveat, healers could help women navigate their fears and concerns. Healers gave women a sense of agency and a sense of hope.

Healers could also deepen family rifts, not least by inserting their own ideas of family into the treatments they prescribed. In migratory Calakmul, the question of the future of marriage hinged very much on perspective. Young and old, women and men had different notions of men's and women's marital roles in the new migratory order. When healers worked at their clients' behest, they reinforced these assorted notions of marriage and family. At the same time, healers were no different from other active stayers in having their own ideas about family.

What made healers distinct was that they might use their entrée to the Otherworldly to enact these notions.

The Otherworldy

Calakmuleños who turned to Berta and other healers took for granted that the visible world—the world in which people go about their daily lives—operated in parallel with an invisible sphere. This invisible sphere was populated by Otherworldly beings. Saints and spirits lived in this hidden dimension, as did malevolent witches. The Otherworldly was also the place where God resided, but from the way Calakmuleños talked about it, the hidden sphere resembled the human world more than it did heaven. It was home to battles between good and evil, just as the human world is.

Beyond this, a simple description of the Otherworldly and how it intersected with everyday life is difficult to produce. Calakmuleños did not elaborate their thoughts on the topic. They did not give the domain a name. Instead, as elsewhere in Mexico, belief in the Otherworldly was a kind of "public secret, shared collectively."[3] Everyone knew about it, but they referred to it only in bits and pieces.

For the most part, people carried on without paying attention to the Otherworldly. Then, some kind of disruption indicated this invisible, yet immanent, sphere had spilled over into the physical realm. An unexplained accident or sickness, poor health that defied the talent of medical doctors—these might signal the Otherworldly in action.

In one case, an emigrant man in Alabama believed he had returned all his family photographs to his wife in Mexico. The two were in the process of divorcing. Unexpectedly, one of the pictures appeared in a photograph frame in his Alabama home. The picture appeared in the very frame he intended for a portrait of himself and his new partner. The photo, he concluded, must have been sent by his wife in Mexico, who used magic to cause it to appear.

Although Calakmuleños did not talk about the Otherworldly in detail, a few observations stand out. One is that they believed the beings living beyond the veil were numerous but sometimes circumscribed in their geography. Some beings could alert a healer to faraway events, but others did not travel the way people did. Thus, Elvia, Rosario, and other Ch'ol people from Chiapas described their home state as populated by fearsome mountain spirits and terrifying, flesh-eating "savages."

These beings did not exist in Calakmul, where relatively benign spirits prevailed in the form of *duendes*. Duendes tried to lure the unwitting into the spirit realm, usually to little effect. The United States seemed to have no Otherworldly beings at all, although from my conversations with migrant men it was unclear whether this absence was because the beings did not exist or because people in the United States did not acknowledge them.

If the worldly and the Otherworldly intersected in the sporadic appearance of beings and other magical phenomena, another meeting place was the human body itself. Calakmuleños understood the body to be occasionally permeable and, therefore, susceptible to mystical infringement. A healer, or a spirit working on a healer's behalf, could take advantage of the body's permeability to act on a person without his or her knowledge. This was how the envious inflicted illness.

The body's permeability was situational and often depended on the character of the person involved. During waking hours, the body was less penetrable because a person's sense of self-control created a barrier to magical intrusion. In general, people with strong personalities were less permeable than the weak-willed. But when people slept or got drunk, they temporarily lost control of themselves, and this loss could provide an opening for healers to act.

Healers like Berta worked at the interface between the visible and Otherworldly, at the point where the body was permeable. Their ability to magically enter another's body, or to use their contacts in the spirit world to do so, was what allowed healers to influence relationships. As Calakmuleños understood things, sometimes the healer aimed to shore up the integrity of the body and ward off an offending intruder. Earlier we learned Selena took a fall which damaged her Achilles' tendon as the result of a neighbor's jealousy (see chapter 3). Rafael suffered a near-blinding headache when his paramour inflicted an imperceptible enchantment on him (see chapter 3). In both cases, a spiteful antagonist took advantage of the body's permeability to exact retribution for some perceived slight. With these sorts of illnesses, healers worked to expel the offending intrusion from the body.

More generally, curanderos used a mystical path into the body to bring two people closer together, force them apart, or create a tolerable coexistence. In other words, healers attempted to act through the Otherworldly to bring about the relationship boundaries their clients desired. The changes to gender and kinship produced by migration naturally altered the boundaries between family members. By turning to healers, active stayers could restore relationships to their proper order. Healthy family boundaries created healthy bodies, and healthy bodies were a sign of harmonious family relationships.

However, because family members differed in their preferred relationship boundaries, Berta and others could also reinforce migration's tendency to trigger family arguments. The people who turned to healers knew curanderos enforced relationship ideals surreptitiously, through the Otherworldly. The secrecy itself opened the door to accusations of witchcraft, which quite predictably could undermine the search for family harmony. In Calakmul and elsewhere, one person's healing was another person's sorcery. Thus, the healing Berta offered was never straightforward, and its value, as well as its efficacy, was often in the eye of the beholder.

Healing at Berta's House

The day Berta showed me her notebooks, we sat in the room her clients first entered when they stepped into her house from the street. Outside, the tropical sun cast a blinding white light. Inside, where the white walls had faded to gray, Berta's reception area was luminous.

At first glance, the space was indistinguishable from other Calakmul homes. The room had obviously been remodeled over the years to allow for extra space. The clapboard walls, corrugated zinc roofing, and cement flooring suggested the house was built by Berta's husband or sons. Home-building with these materials was a common skill among campesino men (and one of the reasons men adapted so easily to construction jobs in the United States).

An altar in the corner of Berta's reception area signaled her uncommon status. Many campesinos hung a crucifix or a saint's image in their home. But Berta had staged a flashy display. Built atop an ordinary table, the altar drew attention with its backdrop of a Mexican flag, a string of lights, and a banner of colored, cut-out paper. Its most prominent feature was a three-foot-tall, framed depiction of the Virgin of Guadalupe, a mother who hears the cries of her suffering children and Mexico's most revered saint. The Virgin floated above sixteen figurines arrayed at her feet. In addition to a crucifix, Berta had displayed two versions of the baby Jesus standing with arms outstretched as if anticipating an embrace. Two sets of nativity scenes depicted six wise men, two Virgin Marys, and two Josephs watching over two infant Jesuses. A second image of the

FIGURE 7.1

The altar before which Berta prayed to alleviate women's troubles. Healers like Berta helped women make sense of migration. If globalization operated through a hidden dimension, Calakmuleños used prayer to access another set of hidden powers that might, God willing, counteract migration's many afflictions.

Photo: Nora Haenn

Virgin of Guadalupe, this one a two-foot statue, also formed part of the mix. To the sides of the altar, Berta had arranged flowering plants, holy water, and two cases of Eternal Light candles (Figure 7.1).

The altar alerted Berta's visitors to her brand of healing power. Healers in Calakmul espoused multiple approaches, although these had sufficient overlap that people tended to view healers as operating within a common tradition.[4] Unlike Samuel, Berta did not profess to have access to a mystical screen. She was, however, similar to Samuel in claiming the aid of spirit guides. She was also similar to other healers in describing her ability to cure as a gift from God. Recounting her past successes, she ended each story by exclaiming, "¡Santa curación!" ("a blessed recovery!").

Calakmuleños had easy access to doctors and nurses employed by an expansive state medical agency. Despite this availability, they remained keen on Berta's prayer-based healing. After all, doctors and nurses could not cure relationships under strain, a point Berta was sure to reinforce. "With the sickness you have, the doctors will just want to operate," she counseled her clients, "but that will not be remedy enough." If anything, the presence of medically trained professionals increased consumption of health care services overall—including the services of curanderos. People carefully assessed the range of healing approaches available. They noticed that Calakmul's professionally trained medical providers viewed themselves as culturally distinct from—sometimes superior to—the poor and largely Indigenous population they served. In Berta, campesinos found respect and cultural understanding.

While I scanned her notebooks, Berta tutored me in the nature of her gift. Anyone, she explained, might recite prayers, but this was not the same as having the power of prayer. The prayers Berta uttered before her altar came from a collection of esoteric religious books. The books included the names of six beneficial spirits who helped transform Berta's speech into divine intercession. Berta was unsure why, but she understood that she had a special ability, a power in and of itself, to unleash the strength within the prayers.

Her work with one client in particular convinced her of the exceptional quality of her talent. He had been so impressed with Berta's work that he wanted to invoke the spirits himself. "So I sat him in a chair before the altar and blessed him," Berta recalled. "We finished praying a psalm, and there he remained. Palid. He couldn't speak. He later said he wanted to vomit. He invoked spirits he shouldn't have. Not just anybody can do this work."

How did Berta know what to pray for? Some of her clients brought specific petitions. "More than anything else, the wives are looking for their husbands to send more money," she responded when I asked if wives sought her help in having their husbands return home. "No, they do not ask to have their husbands return. Why would they want that if he's not going to bring any money? I know how to make people return, but they don't ask for that."

If a husband stopped sending money, Berta averred, a wife might change her mind. When the money stopped flowing, wives asked themselves, " 'What's he doing there? He should just come home.' And then, yes," Berta confirmed,

> I can make a man return. There are special candles and special prayers to bring a person back from the United States. With that prayer, the person would have to come home; nothing will stop him. Because, listen, in the name of the Lord, he has to come, he *has* to come. He has no choice. And, he'll come quickly.

Other clients brought to Berta mysterious maladies that required diagnosis. Her examination entailed first passing an egg over the client's
body while she recited a psalm. Then, she broke the egg into a bowl and
examined the yolk and egg white for signs of witchcraft. If sorcery was
involved, Berta went on to quiz her client about a possible culprit. Was
the woman arguing with anyone? Had she recently had an odd encoun-
ter with someone? Did the client have long-standing enemies?

Questions like these were almost sure to locate the source of ailment in a friend, neighbor, or family member. Suspicions of foul play
by someone near to them were often what brought people to Berta in
the first place. In migratory Calakmul, this line of questioning quickly
brought to light family conflicts arising from a man's absence. Given
how, under the best of circumstances, relations between mothers-in-
law and daughters-in-law could be fraught, Berta's questioning easily
revealed these tensions. Women's fears of abandonment by a husband
or son also existed long before international migration, and Berta could
swiftly expose this concern as well.

While Berta's questioning had predictable aspects, this type of
healing also holds a deeper purpose.[5] By answering Berta's questions,
women crafted stories that made sense of the emotional pain surrounding migration. They gave a story to their suffering.

The stories compensated for the way much about what
Calakmuleños were experiencing was maddening and difficult to put
to words. Family members with the best of intentions found themselves at odds with one another for reasons they could not understand.
Mothers-in-law were sincerely aghast at their daughters-in-law's financial and sexual independence. To mothers-in-law, the younger women's
autonomy betrayed the trust of their emigrant sons. Daughters-in-law
were horror-stricken that their in-laws would respond to their need to
live as something other than a Black Widow with accusations of prof-
ligacy and infidelity. Embattled daughters-in-law found themselves on
the defensive, forced to fight above all for their absent husbands' affection and trust. Both groups of women feared intensely for an absent
man's well-being.

Migration's effects could feel irrational and inexplicable, and Berta
helped women give definition to these sensations while providing a path
to healing. Naming an affliction and its protagonist was a first step in
crafting a narrative and accompanying ritual that returned a person to
health. Knowing the root of an illness allowed Berta to choose among a

range of rituals that might transform a story of misfortune into a story of remedy and repair.

As part of her healing magic, Berta might burn a colored candle, brush a person with aromatic herbs, or prescribe a dose of holy water. Depending on the case, her prayers might need reinforcement. If the object of her prayers lived at a distance, she might ask for a photograph or an article of the person's clothing. The connection to a physical object facilitated her efforts. When Berta prayed for a man living in the United States, she often kneeled before her altar in the pre-dawn hours, when the target of her intercession was likely to be asleep. After traveling the considerable distance, her words had a greater chance of entering a man's body if his self-control were suspended.

The healthy bodies that Berta nurtured evidenced peace between people and accord between the Otherworldly and the everyday. But Berta was always careful to strike a cautionary note: her work depended on God's will, and God answered some prayers but not others. In some cases, an unhealthy body or a frayed relationship reflected God's mysterious plans about which there was nothing much she or her clients could do.

Given these vagaries, Berta instructed all the clients who visited her home not to talk about her healing efforts until their problem was resolved. Berta did not want to raise false expectations. And despite her power of prayer, her faith in the saints that populated her altar, and her mystical connection to the spirit world, Berta's prayers might go unanswered if God had other intentions.

When I asked Berta about mothers-in-law and daughters-in-law, I touched on a topic she had carefully considered. Relations between these women could be so difficult, she believed, that without the intervention of a healer like herself, they were unlikely to improve. Daughters-in-law came to Berta complaining their mothers-in-law fed false rumors to their sons in an effort to get the men to stop sending money to their wives. The daughters-in-law asked Berta to cast a charm on their husbands "so they'll no longer pay attention to their mothers." In contrast, mothers-in-law accused their daughters-in-law of dating other men: "And, as a mother-in-law myself, if I knew that my son was suffering to earn money while his wife was out looking for another man, well, I wouldn't want that either."

Berta described her work on behalf of mothers-in-law. To cast a charm on a daughter-in-law, Berta lit a blue candle that offered the older woman "protection," comparable to the kind of protection she secured for someone who feared witchcraft. Here, Berta was quick to say that while much witchcraft centered on jealousy over money, this particular protection was not at all money-related. Berta seemed to want to assure me that mothers-in-law were not simply out to grab the remittances, as their daughters-in-law protested. Instead, Berta emphasized that the protection she offered gave mothers-in-law a general ability to prevent harm to their families.

After lighting the blue candle, Berta took out a piece of paper and wrote the daughter-in-law's name on it. On the same paper, she copied out the name of the mother-in-law, making sure to cover the letters of the younger woman's name with the letters of the older woman's name. The next step in the curing entailed bathing the paper in honey or sugar. Reciting prayers as she went along, Berta offered the paper up to God.

As a result of the charm, Berta claimed the daughter-in-law stopped pressuring her husband to send more money than he was already remitting. The woman also lost the desire to speak. For Berta, a silenced daughter-in-law meant the younger woman "behaved as a better person with her mother-in-law." As in other patriarchal societies, Berta thought "a good wife was one who learned how to be quiet"[6] both with her husband and with her mother-in-law.

Berta's advocacy for mothers-in-law left me wondering what exactly she did for the daughters-in-law who sought her aid. "How do you respond when a young woman asks you to make her husband no longer listen to his mother?" I ventured.

"I almost never do that kind of work," Berta replied. "You know why? Because it's bad to make a son hate his mother. Because this is his mother. I tell the daughter-in-law I will do that, but I won't. It's just wrong. Working against the mother-in-law is wrong. Many young women have come to me with this request. What I will do is separate the two women. I will have the daughter-in-law live elsewhere. That way the arguments stop." Berta assumed the daughter-in-law in this hypothetical case lived in patrilocal residence.

Berta's answer suggested she was less than straightforward with the daughters-in-law who sought her help. Did the younger women know Berta used her prayers to encourage a separation? I asked. Contradicting her earlier statement, Berta confirmed the daughters-in-law were aware of her intentions, but I was not so sure. Berta's story had changed very quickly.

I continued with another topic: "And if a young wife asked for help in having her husband send money to her and not to his mother, would that be okay?" This, Berta said, she was willing to do: "Allí, sí está bien," "Yes, that's alright." Again, I was unsure of the claim. Her support for mothers-in-law suggested Berta ascribed to older ideas of marriage that premised a submissive daughter-in-law.

I decided not to probe this inconsistency. As a public figure, Berta was adept at self-presentation. And because she assumed I was an admirer of her work, in the way newspaper and radio interviewers had been before, I sensed our conversation could become very uncomfortable if I pointed out irregularities in her story. In any case, Berta had years of practice in keeping secrets. If Berta had a secret of her own about how she healed families, I was unlikely to learn it.

Notes

1. Lindquist 2006: 4.
2. See Carling in Levitt and Jaworsky 2007: 138.
3. Pitarch 2010: 12. Pitarch's research on healing in Chiapas elucidates the Otherworldly as understood by Elvia and healers in her family.
4. See Nemogá Soto 2004.
5. Lindquist 2006; Pitarch 2010; Turner 1982.
6. Menjívar 2011: 82.

....

CHAPTER 8

Bringing It All Home

I n the early 2000s, a rumor circulated around Calakmul. This one did not focus on a particular married couple but on the institution of marriage itself. The rumor asserted that a first marriage lasted forever regardless of whatever came next. Long-lasting marriages, some people said, were part of God's greater plan. Come the Last Judgment— after the Second Coming of Christ and the resurrection of the dead— people who had divorced, separated, or remarried would be reunited with their original spouse for all of eternity. When God's justice was finally enacted, the story affirmed, there would be no divorce or marital separation. The rumor did not implicate international migration directly, but the message was clear. The reunification would apply to people whose marriages ended because of migration-related disputes or the simple fact of physical separation. God's final justice would undo the damage migration had done.

For anthropologists, rumors such as this one help people "explain uncertain, ambiguous events or intangible fears."[1] Rumors, especially strange ones, are a sign people are struggling with an issue vital to their community. Without trustworthy or reliable information, gossip and rumor give people a way to test out ideas that might make sense of things.

Rumors about marriage and the marital behavior of husbands and wives served an essential function for Calakmuleños as they traversed migration's pleasures and dangers. Global structures such as men's labor migration rely on contact with local counterparts in order to exist. Yet whether they traveled or remained at home, Calakmuleños could not see many of the forces they were running up against. Although they were well aware of the class and ethnic tensions that placed campesinos and Indigenous people at the bottom of Mexico's social ladder, the distant drivers of migration—such as NAFTA, Mexican federal policy, and the actions of US employers and policymakers—were beyond their line of sight. Instead, Calakmuleños felt migration's most immediate impact on their marriages. Rumor and gossip allowed Calakmuleños to assess marriage as a site of friction that gave migration a degree of locomotion. [2]

When local and global meet, the two elements change each other, but local and global rarely meet on an even playing field.[3] Despite their pleasures, global structures can expose people already marginalized in their access to resources, information, and power to repeated harm. When this happens, global structures enact a structural violence, a violence people suffer as intimate and personal.

As Calakmuleños experienced it, part of the structural violence of migration was that they did not have the political or economic sway to determine its course. They could not control the pleasurable and the dangerous dynamics migration put into motion. They could not control the love and loss that accompanied migration. Gossip about marriage and migration was one way active stayers used their repertoire to exert a limited, collective power. Gossip allowed people to bring women's immobility and men's mobility into a single conversation. Through rumor and innuendo, Calakmuleños pushed back against people's personal behavior, while simultaneously carving out a role for personal decision making within the larger social dynamic created by Mexico and the United States's integrated labor market.

In this meeting ground of global structure, local repertoire, and personal choice, the idea that men traveled to meet family goals— Calakmuleños' collective, agreed upon notion of migration's pleasures— served as a meta-solution. The claim smoothed over the inevitable abrasions and provided a moral framework for why mobility and immobility should accompany one another in the first place.

In actuality, men traveled for a variety of reasons. The promise of much higher earnings in the United States was important. But some men were simply curious, others wanted to escape family and community life. Like the US tourists who visit Calakmul, for some young Calakmuleños international travel was a romantic thrill that could send chills down the spine. Reflecting on his thoughts before leaving Zarajuato at the age of sixteen, one young roofer in Alabama recalled dreaming at night of crossing the desert and being chased by US border patrol. He also dreamed of owning cars: "Oh, I imagined things would be very different. I thought I would have a house in Mexico with lots of rooms and five cars. I thought that would happen quickly."

It wasn't always clear to what extent women were participants in deciding that migration was the best path to achieve family goals. Some men traveled against their wives' wishes.[4] Others were pressured by their wives, who wanted the boost in income or their own break from married life. Plenty of families became involved in migration for the simple reason that lots of people were doing it. Migration was a kind of fashion. By claiming they traveled to meet family goals, travelers and the active stayers who supported them evoked gender norms to cultivate a veneer of acceptability regardless of their underlying intentions.

By "family" goals, Calakmuleños often meant marital goals. And as Selena's and Rosario's financial savvy showed, one goal people regularly talked about was that of "pulling the family ahead." The idea sounded a lot like the American Dream, but it came with Calakmuleños' own formula for success. Migrant families, people said, should build a house, open a shop, or invest remittances in some other family-based business. Like their reasons for traveling, these public proclamations could mask a range of goals, including some that aimed to change family life by bolstering young people's ability to live outside patrilocal residence. When their financial goals emphasized a working, homebound wife, Calakmuleños attempted to address dilemmas posed by their notions of feminine honor. These ideals hampered women's entrepreneurial energies and limited their income-earning possibilities.

Families and their goals, however, came undone when migration resulted in a marriage's demise. Calakmuleños feared that emigrant men might marry while abroad and turn their attentions to their new family, as did the husbands of both Aurora and Rosario. Understandably, men who traveled as bachelors might find a spouse wherever they landed. As for married men, Calakmuleños had a list of reasons why they might remarry or acquire a second wife: the men were philandering louses; the United States was a land of perversity where men could lose their way; the men's wives in Mexico were profligate adulterers who gave the travelers little reason to return. By curing men of the siren lure of women who used magic to tie migrants to the United States, the healer Samuel proposed that the problem with migration was the way it behaved as a beguiling captor. Its pleasures were inextricably bound with its dangers.

Popular opinion was notably silent on the role mothers-in-law such as Elvia played in all this. Mothers-in-law also counted among the family an emigrant man might support. And because they relied on sons in their old age, mothers had a keen interest in the quality of their sons' marriages, including the younger couple's financial life. Under patrilocal residence, relations between mothers-in-law and daughters-in-law lent themselves to tension. In the era of international migration, conflicts between a mother-in-law and a daughter-in-law were potent enough to end a marriage.

Why were Calakmuleños silent about the older women's influence? I believe their avoidance stemmed from a few causes. Calakmuleños continued to assign women, rather than men, the burden of upholding gender norms and keeping their marriages together. Thus, they placed the blame for marital troubles on young wives and paramours rather than on the senior generation. Another part of Calakmuleños' repertoire that still received broad support was the notion that older women deserved respect and deference. Many young people hesitated to criticize older women they viewed as long-suffering. Young men, especially those accustomed to their mothers' indulgence, were often genuinely flummoxed when a doting parent transformed into their marriages' meddling adversary.

By gossiping about couples engaged in migration, and not about larger family dynamics, Calakmuleños emphasized the way migration gained traction by fostering new gender ideals and new marital bargains. These new marriages reconfigured the role of young wives, making it possible for some women to claim amusements formerly reserved for men. Model migrant wives like Selena did not take this course; they scrupulously guarded their reputation for modesty. An exemplary migrant wife might, as one did, buy ranchland but then protest she could not possibly carry out a man's job by tending the cattle. The claim invoked older ideas of marriage as a working partnership and pressured the husband to return and resume his share of the workload.

In contrast, women such as Aurora sought to take advantage of their husbands' absence to expand their freedoms. They traveled unchaperoned and went as far as spending money in the pursuit of sexual freedom. By having an extramarital affair or acquiring a second spouse, these young women thumbed their noses at the old double standards that denied them romance. These freedoms were not an unqualified good. Some women feared a husband's abandonment and felt forced into new relationships, marginal jobs, and other stigmatized situations. Other women were expanding their freedoms by taking timid, modest steps. Given the straitjacketed life Calakmuleños expected of young wives, it could sometimes be hard to tell whether young women's actions were a positive claim to social change or an escape from enforced widowhood.

The changes to Calakmuleños' repertoire surrounding gender were radical, but in reality, migration chafed against old and new ideals alike. Young couples turned to migration to relieve the stressors of patrilocal residence. Here, local history and the local repertoire matter, as elsewhere researchers have found men's labor migration can reinforce patrilocal norms.[5] In Calakmul, migration gave young husbands a conventional, temporary escape from their extended families. Meanwhile, for young women, one of migration's disappointments was that they did not enjoy a comparable freedom.

A young woman may have thought emigration would speed her along the path to independent living. Instead, a husband's departure brought her intense family scrutiny, in a way reinserting her into the tension-filled aspects of patrilocal residence that the young couple sought to escape. Personal decision-making and preferences could markedly affect this aspect of the migratory journey. In her work, for example, Deborah Boehm met a mother-in-law and daughter-in-law who shared a warm friendship. The two women enjoyed living together such that when the absent husband divorced his wife, the women grieved their resulting separation.[6]

Under these circumstances, young women found themselves in a position of double jeopardy. As financial managers charged with implementing a family's migratory goals, it was unavoidable that young wives would take the lead in creating culture change. Yet as kin keepers, women were also tasked with protecting the existing social order.

The two jobs proved nearly impossible to combine. Calakmuleños sought a better life from migration, but family differences raised the question of "a better life for whom?" Did "better" mean an improved version of what Calakmuleños already had? Mothers-in-law and other active stayers advocated this position. Or did "better" mean emphasizing new aspects of their repertoire? Young wives and others of their generation advocated this contrary viewpoint. International migration on its own could not settle the question of who got to define and mete out migration's pleasures and dangers.

For women such as Selena, Aurora, and Rosario, their problems were exacerbated by expectations that they would heed a distant husband's authority. Some men saw this prerogative as a natural extension of their patriarchal privilege. One husband I knew telephoned from the United States to refuse his wife medical treatment. The wife had a gynecological problem, and the husband assumed she had faked the illness in order to access birth control: he believed that medically recommended contraceptives would have allowed his wife to carry out an extramarital affair without risk of pregnancy. Calakmul's rumor mill guaranteed the woman's family and neighbors also knew of his decision, so any action on her part would require standing up to both her husband and the public pressure that backed his authority.

Nowhere were the simultaneoulsy changing and enduring qualities of gender relations more visible than in home construction. Under older marital norms, young husbands built the houses they and their wives lived in, a practical act that was also symbolic. The house belonged to him, but the fact of shared residence made it a collective endeavor. In the era of international migration, many Calakmuleño men stopped building houses for their wives. Instead, they built for people in the United States. Wives oversaw construction of the new, dollar-based houses in Calakmul, often contracting their own father or brothers to carry out the work. Houses, and the kind of sharing required to build and maintain them, changed radically with men's labor migration. Yet women's far away husbands remained entitled to direct details of their wives' day-to-day lives. Women's homes were still not their own (Figure 8.1).

The situation left women in a bind, and wives with partners increasingly out of touch with family life incurred considerable penalties for rebuffing their husbands. A husband's mother was often on hand to act as her son's enforcer. Older women sought to maintain their emotional bond to their sons, in part because they wanted access to his earnings. A remitting son might be an older woman's only chance for financial security. Meanwhile, a young wife who failed to do as her husband wished feared losing him to a stateside wife or to her mother-in-law. Another point of friction in men's labor migration was the way it created competition between women over men.

For women and men alike, a husband's return was no guarantee that the hazards of migration's structural violence would end. At the

FIGURE **8.1**

Three houses reveal changing social relations in Calakmul. The house on the left, made of cement block, is the sort typically built with money earned by migration. The house in the middle was also erected in the 2000s. Part of a government housing initiative, its design was stipulated by the program. The house on the right is a shotgun style house self-consciously modeled after similar company homes in the United States. This last style of construction was originally brought to Calakmul in the 1950s by a local timber baron.
Photo: Nora Haenn

least, married couples underwent a period of re-acquaintance. They had to bridge the many kinds of separations that sprang up between them after years of living apart. Women who remained at home could hardly comprehend the perils of a desert crossing, life and work in a country where English predominated, the stressors of undocumented living, and other aspects of men's sojourns. Men who traveled did not share women's odysseys in raising children as a single parent, handling remittances, or enduring local gossip. Of the two, women had the greater disadvantage. Women knew less about men's migratory experiences than men knew about women's, a fact exacerbated by men's colluding to keep their stateside lives a secret.

In worst-case scenarios, migration's structural violence translated into a physical violence directed toward women like Rosario and Aurora.

Domestic violence is often associated with economic dislocation, and with a migrant's return families could easily undergo a 90 percent loss in income. A man who earned $500 to $1,000 a week in the United States would be hard-pressed to find full-time employment in Calakmul that paid $75 to $150 a week. Migrants who returned to farming might wait months before their harvests paid out and, then, at incredibly low prices. In the meantime, climate change has made farming even more unpredictable in Calakmul. [7]

Returning to Mexico also marked an end to men's life of stateside self-indulgence. Calakmuleños viewed the United States as a land of partying, one great big cantina where men reveled in masculine pleasures. But drinking was also a way men coped with stressors, including migration-induced trauma. When men returned home, migration's immediate afflictions might evaporate, but a physical addiction to alcohol or the habit of turning to drink to escape problems might continue. For some men, migration worsened the problem drinking that triggered or escalated domestic violence.

Domestic violence was just one example of how women's migratory odysseys in Mexico and men's sojourns abroad inevitably interacted with one another. Women's immobility and men's mobility were each their own kind of journey that were impossible to separate from one another.[8] At a very basic level, Calakmuleños expected migration to change a married couple. Their ideas of migration as a way to "pull the family ahead" evidences their hopes that migration would transform families. At a deeper level, Calakmuleños expected migration would bring about mutual transformation because they viewed family members as essential to one another's very being.

"You live alone?" Elvia asked me during the early days of our friendship. "You're not afraid to live alone?" For the anthropologist Marshall Sahlins, Elvia's understanding that nobody should ever live without kin is characteristic of how people everywhere think about family. People inherit some family relations upon birth; people also create kin through co-habitation, marriage, adoption, and the creation of fictive kin. Godparents, blood brothers, sorority sisters, close family friends who earn the title of "aunt" or "uncle," these are just some of the family people make as relations grow cherished over time. The intimacy of these family ties makes them different from relationships such as neighbors, friends, coworkers, or employers. For Sahlins, kin ties are unique because even if people's time together is brief or sporadic, the relationship is dense. Kin *presume* their lives are interwoven. "Relatives," Sahlins writes, "emotionally and symbolically live each other's lives and die each other's deaths."[9]

Calakmul's healers might aver that family members also live each other's illness. When migration caused family relationships to become abrasive, migration made people sick. For Berta and her clients, illness was a surface manifestation of hidden connections that transcended space. Like anthropological theories of kinship, Calakmuleños' notion that an invisible sphere existed apart from the physical realm pointed to a sharing that physical distance could not easily displace. Before the advent of international migration, Calakmuleños turned to the Otherworldly to affect the concealed dimensions of family ties. In the face of migration's own hidden drivers, Calakmuleños emphasized people's personal, migration-related decisions, and they returned to the Otherworldly to influence one another's behavior. Despite their different notions of what family harmony looked like, Calakmuleños shared a common concern that migration not cause family members to drift apart.

At the beginning of this book, I explained that Elvia, Selena, Aurora, Rosario, and Berta formed part of a "migrant network." They were part of a network because they all knew each other or knew of each other. I made this assertion in order to connect the women to a popular way of thinking about international migration, namely migrant network theory. Migrant networks are webs of people—sprawling and overlapping collections of friends, family, and neighbors—that span sending and receiving communities.[10] Research on migrant networks tends to focus on migrants themselves, suggesting the people who can best explain how and why migration takes place are the people who travel. In this way, the theory mirrors popular understandings of Mexican migration in the United States that overwhelmingly focus on migrants residing in the North.

As one critic of migrant network theory notes, this focus leaves out other people who make migration possible.[11] Setting aside for the moment the authors of NAFTA and migration's other distant drivers, the theory—along with popular punditry in the United States—can overlook the US employers of immigrants, the recruiting agents who travel in search of workers, the smugglers who guide people across the border, the landlords who rent to immigrants, and countless others. In situations of men's labor migration, an emphasis on travelers leaves out the women and others who stay put and, thereby, help shape migratory outcomes.

Although the lines between who counts as a mover and who counts as an active stayer are not always neatly drawn, in general in order for some people to be mobile, others must be immobile. In order for some people to find privilege in staying put or privilege in traveling, others must be stigmatized for doing the opposite.[12] And when migratory flows multiply, people still denigrate some kinds of travel in order to reserve other kinds as a marker of high status.[13] NAFTA, for example, has come to stand as an exemplar of state policies across the world that first increase the flow of migrant workers and then categorize these travelers as "undocumented" or "illegal."[14] By failing to expand the migrant network beyond travelers, we miss out on these important dimensions.

What do we learn by including women and active stayers in migrant networks and seeing things from their standpoint? Compare how network theory describes migration's start with men's travels as Calakmuleños' knew them. Migrant network theory posits that international migration begins when a few intrepid souls make the trip. These pioneers return with stories of high-paying jobs. They offer knowledge and finances to entice prospective travelers. As the stream of travelers grows, outmigration becomes widespread until what started as a slow drip becomes a torrent. If the torrent lasts long enough, new sending communities might develop a culture of migration.[15] Travel for work becomes an expected and essential part of social life.

Women and active stayers in Calakmul would probably agree with this story in broad strokes, but they might point out details the theory glosses over.

Calakmuleños supported men's travels as a way to meet family goals. Women's role as active stayers was always an essential counterpart to men's sojourns. Women and men in Calakmul believed men's work in the United States would be compatible with family life as they knew it, because they had generations of experience with men's temporary labor migration. For centuries, men's travel for work was required by Mexican state officials. When these demands ended, men's off-farm earnings continued to sustain campesino families. In the run up to international migration, Calakmuleño marriages survived additional kinds of migration. These included multiple relocations within Mexico and, for some, flight from civil war.

One reason their marriages endured was because married couples did not live in isolation from each other. Married couples depended on and drew support from a dense web of family relationships, of which patrilocal residence was emblematic.

The women might explain that once international migration was underway, they became acquainted with some of its hidden aspects. But they never grasped its dynamics fully, because parts of migration's expansive structure remained concealed to them. It was after international migration got its start that Calakmuleños learned this new round of labor migration was *not* like their previous travels.

International migration altered women's roles by expanding their responsibilities.[16] But international travel also brought them more money and more pleasures than they ever imagined. The money helped propel changes to gender norms. In order to spend the cash and meet those family goals, young women had to break with gender ideals. They knew that with money to spend on partying and extramarital affairs, men in the United States were exaggerating their gender privileges. Some young women saw no reason why they shouldn't share in the fun.

Calakmuleños' tendency to conflate romance with a disposable income enhanced the atmosphere of sexual frisson. Romance and consumerism reinforced each other to make marriage more fragile. Marriages built around the shared workload of farming—which offered few avenues to divorce—were well positioned to withstand men's absences. Marriages in which migration was linked to the idea that wedded life should bring personal satisfaction were vulnerable to dissolution.[17]

Senior women might protest that they tried to put a lid on these changes, and if the old system of patrilocal residence were firmly in place, they might have prevailed. The women might have exerted their authority over younger couples to manage the gender changes and competition over remittances. With a mother-in-law at the helm, men's sojourns might still have transformed into a culture of migration. As we saw, mothers had their own reasons for wanting a son employed and sending money. But, the women might argue, the marital strife would have been lessened. Which is to say, mothers-in-law would have promoted smoother migratory journeys on both sides of the border by having their daughters-in-law pay the price in submissiveness.[18]

In all, the women would probably argue that men traveled to the United States to secure money for their families. If men stayed in the United States, or if they continued to migrate back and forth, their reasons for doing so still tended to center on marriage. Men who remained in the United States might do so because they became "lost," or because they wed and settled down there. Men might forever reside north of the border after their marriage in Mexico fell apart, leaving them nothing to return to.

A life of circular migration resolved other marital problems that arose almost immediately after Calakmuleños joined the migration stream. Becoming reacquainted with one's spouse after years of separation could be painful. A man accustomed to fulfilling the role of family provider with a US salary faced disgrace when a weak job market in Mexico returned his family to poverty. In either case, it was just easier on the couple to keep traveling.

Eight years after the Great Recession forced many Calakmuleño men out of the United States and back to their homes in Mexico, word got around that opportunity may have returned to the US job market. The few Calakmuleños who had chosen to stay in the United States telephoned their brothers, uncles, sons, and other relatives. The stateside men lured their relatives with promises of hourly pay ranging from nine to sixteen dollars. For nearly a decade, wages in Calakmul had hardly budged from seven dollars a day. International trade agreements continued to disadvantage campesinos, so returns from farming were similarly stagnant.[19] And while some aspects of life in Calakmul were inexpensive, others were surprisingly costly. When Elvia or Rosario traveled two hours to the county's market town, she paid half a day's wage per person for public transportation. The more low-cost clothing lines charged a similar amount for a pair of jeans or a skirt. Federal policies that eroded the incomes of Mexico's smallholding farmers continued to have their effect. Meanwhile, for a variety of reasons US employers in construction, farming, hospitality, and other sectors still relied on immigrant labor, as did the larger US economy.

An income of ten, twenty, thirty times what they might earn in Mexico was incentive enough to migrate, but Calakmuleños on both sides of the border now counted family reunification among their reasons to travel. With kin split between two countries, some family members felt isolated and alone. Migration could create "perpetual mourners"[20] of family members permanently separated, and this was not what Calakmuleños wanted for themselves.

Women approached the prospect of renewed migration warily. The savings families had accumulated in previous migrations had been spent down over the years. But this round of migration was, again, men's labor migration, and women had not forgotten the lessons of the past. Now in their thirties and forties, these wives had entered a new phase of life, and this influenced their thinking. Age had given these women greater bargaining power in their communities and in their marriages. Such power placed them in a better position to resist a husband's migration if they wanted.[21] *A few wives, whose marriages had survived earlier bouts of separation, calculated the odds their matrimony would endure another years-long split and decided they had learned how to ensure their marriages persevered. The women's mothers-in-law no longer loomed over them as authority figures. Some had become mothers-in-law in their own right. Overall, the women who had once contended with gossip were freer to run their households as they saw fit. Age also left these wives at liberty to contemplate travels of their own. If their marriages came into jeopardy, they just might join their husbands in the United States.*[22]

After a few of the seasoned migrators risked the trip again, the response from neighboring active stayers was swift. In addition to envy-related witchcraft, this time around people involved in migration complained the junior men in their families were the target of gossip campaigns. Ironically, the more successful a man's migration was financially, the greater the pressure on his younger relatives to travel. "Nothing you have is yours," friends and relatives taunted the sons, sons-in-law, and other male dependents of migrant men. "You live off your father/father-in-law/grandfather."

The humiliation stoked some young men's desire to earn their own dollars in order to pay for their own houses. One hallmark of a culture of migration is that travel becomes a rite of passage that transforms youth into men.[23] *The way Calakmuleños saw things, men were husbands or future husbands. This pressure suggested Calakmuleños had begun to envision marriage as requiring men's separation from their wives in order to maintain families of their own. The earlier wave of migration had helped change Calakmuleños' marital bargains to include ideas of romance and consumerism. Young couples continued to see romance in a life replete with consumer trappings. And a man's emigration was still the quickest path for a young couple to secure this life. As women's expectations about what a man should provide increased, marriage became more costly, a point which placed even more pressure on young men to migrate.*

Calakmuleños continued to view marriage as a bulwark against migration's tendency to sunder family ties. In one case, when a young married man insisted on migrating, the elder generation pressured the young couple to legalize their relationship by securing a state-issued marriage certificate. The two had been living juntado, or joined in matrimony. Their elders considered this bond insufficient to the task. The young woman's parents, in particular, viewed a legal marriage as assurance their son-in-law was not traveling with the intention of abandoning his wife.

As before, in this tentative renewal of migratory flows, only a minority of Calakmuleños participated in the international sojourns. Neighbors and family discouraged one another from traveling by telling stories of deadly desert crossings and the specter of a life lived outside the law. They watched TV news of anti-immigrant sentiment in the United States and took note of the changing politics. I listened as Calakmuleño friends brought a

FIGURE 8.2
A family reunited after years of caring for each other from across international borders.
Photo: Nora Haenn

slightly sharper edge to a question they had put to me often: Why could I move between the United States and Mexico with ease while they could not?

Nonetheless, the outflow was sufficiently widespread to suggest international migration had taken root within Calakmuleños' repertoire. People had come to view migration as one way to compensate for local economic conditions and afford married life (Figure 8.2). And with family members on both sides of the border, Calakmuleños had also come to view migration as a way to maintain the family ties that were now as globalized as the migration that brought Calakmuleños to the United States in the first place.

Notes

1. Samper 2002: 4.
2. To gain a clearer understanding of the density of information circulating around Calakmul, as well as the demand for such information, consider the following: When Facebook became available in the county, enterprising journalists set up news pages. Two of these secured some 8,000 followers. In a county of 28,000 residents—a number which includes the elderly, children, and people living in communities with limited internet or cell phone access—the figures are high. In my experience, while many of these followers likely live outside the region (as I do), these pages structured daily conversation in Calakmul. People talked about what had been posted, whether the news was accurate, and what might be going on behind the scenes to drive the news.
3. Levitt and Merry 2009.
4. Young wives in particular may have little say in a husband's decision to migrate. Their junior status, inexperience with negotiating power differences in their marriage, and presumptions of men's household authority all bear upon a young woman's ability to identify and voice her migratory preferences. Women gain agency and authority over their own and their family's migration-related decisions as they age (Hondagneu-Sotelo 1994). From my experience, even when young wives did support a first migration, they balked at later trips.
5. See Rao cited in Brettell 2017.
6. Boehm 2012.
7. Rodriguez-Solorzano 2014.
8. Salazar and Smart 2011.
9. Sahlins 2013: ix.

10. Massey et al. 1993.
11. Krissman 2005.
12. Glick Schiller and Salazar 2013; Jónsson 2017; Salazar and Smart 2022.
13. Portes 2000.
14. Coe 2013.
15. Massey et al. 1993; Cohen 2004.
16. Boehm 2008.
17. Coontz 2006.
18. Pessar and Mahler (2003) note the need to further consider the role of patrilocality in migration streams. The Calakmul case shows patrilocality is a key aspect of men's labor migration. Patrilocality intersects with other cultural values, as well as particular migration structures, such that its role in international migration may prove multi-faceted.
19. In late 2018, Mexico and the United States revised NAFTA to create the USMCA or United States-Mexico-Canada Agreement. As of writing, the USMCA awaited congressional approval. However, because the USMCA retained NAFTA's agricultural provisions, it is not expected to change the conditions campesinos face.
20. Ainslie in Zavella 2011: 158.
21. Nobles and McKelvey 2015.
22. In the years following Calakmul's incorporation into international labor flows, out-migration to regional destinations also became popular, especially to Cancún and the Riviera Maya. People said local travel was cheaper and less dangerous than international travel. Migrants could stay in touch with their families through short trips home. Young, unmarried women appeared more likely to participate in internal migration, in part to search for mates. Many young women no longer saw their campesino peers as capable of providing the standard of living they desired (McEvoy et al. 2012).
23. Pribilsky 2007.

WORKS CITED

Adelman, M., 2017. *Battering states: The politics of domestic violence in Israel.* Nashville: Vanderbilt University Press.

Adler, R. H., 2015. *Yucatecans in Dallas, Texas: Breaching the border, bridging the distance.* New York: Routledge.

Aguirre Beltrán, G., 1967. *Regiones de refugio: El desarrollo de la comunidad y el proceso dominical en mestizo América.* Mexico City: Instituto Indigenista Interamericano.

Alejos García, J., 1994. *Mosojäntel: etnografía del discurso agrarista entre los ch'oles de Chiapas.* Mexico City: Universidad Autónoma de México.

Alejos García, J., 1999. *Ch'ol/Kaxlan: Identidades étnicas y conflicto agrario en el norte de Chiapas, 1914–1940.* Mexico City: Universidad Nacional Autónoma de México.

Andrews, A. L., 2018. *Undocumented politics: Place, gender, and the pathways of Mexican migrants.* Berkeley: University of California Press.

Appadurai, A., 1996. *Modernity at large: Cultural dimensions of globalization.* Minneapolis: University of Minnesota Press.

Arana Cedeño, M. and del Riego, M. T., 2012. *Estudio sobre los desplazados por el conflicto armado en Chiapas.* Mexico City: Programa Conjunto por una Cultura de Paz.

Assies, W., 2008. Land tenure and tenure regimes in Mexico: An overview. *Journal of Agrarian Change, 8*(1), 33–63.

Baldez, L., 2004. The gender quota law for legislative candidates in Mexico. *Legislative Studies Quarterly, 29*(2), 231–258.

Benjamin, T., 1989. *A rich land, a poor people: Politics and society in modern Chiapas.* Albuquerque: University of New Mexico Press.

Beres, M. A., 2007. 'Spontaneous' sexual consent: An analysis of sexual consent literature. *Feminism & Psychology, 17*(1), 93–108.

Bobrow-Strain, A., 2007. *Intimate enemies: Landowners, power, and violence in Chiapas*. Durham: Duke University Press.

Boehm, D.A., 2012. *Intimate migrations: Gender, family, and illegality among transnational Mexicans*. New York: New York University Press.

Boehm, D. A., 2008. 'Now I am a man and a woman!' Gendered moves and migrations in a transnational Mexican community. *Latin American Perspectives*, 35(1), 16–30.

Borges, G., Breslau, J., Orozco, R., Tancredi, D. J., Anderson, H., Aguilar-Gaxiola, S. and Mora, M. E. M., 2011. A cross-national study on Mexico-US migration, substance use and substance use disorders. *Drug and Alcohol Dependence*, 117(1), 16–23.

Brettell, C., 1986. *Men who migrate, women who wait: Population and history in a Portuguese parish*. Princeton: Princeton University Press.

Brettell, C., 2016. *Gender and migration*. Cambridge: Polity Press.

Brettell, C., 2017. Marriage and migration. *Annual Review of Anthropology*, 46, 81–97.

Brockington, D. and Igoe, J., 2006. Eviction for conservation: A global overview. *Conservation and Society*, 4(3), 424–470.

Broughton, C., 2008. Migration as engendered practice: Mexican men, masculinity, and northward migration. *Gender & Society*, 22(5), 568–589.

Bourdieu, P., 1992. *The logic of practice*. Palo Alto: Stanford University Press.

Cancian, F., 1994. *The decline of community in Zinacantán: Economy, public life, and social stratification, 1960–1987*. Palo Alto: Stanford University Press.

Cantú, L., 2009. *The Sexuality of migration: Border crossings and Mexican immigrant men*. New York: New York University Press.

Carey Jr., D., 2014. Drunks and dictators: Inebration's gendered, ethnic, and class components in Guatemala, 1898–1944. In *Alcohol in Latin America: A social and cultural history*. Pierce and Toxqui, eds. Tucson: University of Arizona Press, pp. 131–158.

Cardoletti-Carroll, C., Farmer, A., Vélez, L., 2015. *Women on the run: First hand accounts of refugees fleeing El Salvador, Guatemala, Honduras and Mexico*. Washington, DC: United Nations High Commissioner on Refugees.

Carrillo, H., 2017. *Pathways of desire: The sexual migration of Mexican gay men*. Chicago: University of Chicago Press.

Carsten, J., 2004. *After kinship*. Cambridge: Cambridge University Press.

Chavez, L. R., 2001. *Covering immigration: Popular images and the politics of the nation*. Berkeley: University of California Press.

Cliggett, L., 2005. Remitting the gift: Zambian mobility and anthropological insights for migration studies. *Population, Space and Place*, 11(1), 35–48.

Coe, C., 2013. *The scattered family: Parenting, African migrants, and global inequality*. Chicago: University of Chicago Press.

Cohen, D., 2011. *Braceros: Migrant citizens and transnational subjects in the postwar United States and Mexico*. Chapel Hill: University of North Carolina Press.

Cohen, J. H., 2001. Transnational migration in rural Oaxaca, Mexico: Dependency, development, and the household. *American Anthropologist, 103*(4), 954–967.

Cohen, J. H., 2004. *The culture of migration in southern Mexico.* Austin: University of Texas Press.

Cole, J., 2010. *Sex and salvation: Imagining the future in Madagascar.* Chicago: University of Chicago Press.

Cohen, P. 2019. Southerners, facing big odds, believe in a path out of poverty. *New York Times.* https://www.nytimes.com/2019/07/04/business/economy/social-mobility-south.html Accessed July 4, 2019.

Collier, G. A., 2005, 3rd ed. *Basta!: Land and the Zapatista rebellion in Chiapas.* Oakland: Food First Books.

Collier, J. F. and Yanagisako, S. J., 1987. *Gender and kinship: Essays toward a unified analysis.* Palo Alto: Stanford University Press.

Constable, N. 2009. The commodification of intimacy: Marriage, sex, and reproductive labor. *Annual Review of Anthropology, 38,* 49–64.

Coontz, S., 2006. *Marriage, a history: How love conquered marriage.* New York: Penguin.

Cornelius, W. A., 2001. Death at the border: Efficacy and unintended consequences of US immigration control policy. *Population and Development Review, 27*(4), 661–685.

Crawford, D. 2019. *Dealing with privilege: Cannabis, cocaine, and the economic foundations of suburban drug culture.* Lanham: Rowman & Littlefield.

Davies, S. G., 2007. *Challenging gender norms: Five genders among Bugis in Indonesia.* New York: Wadsworth Publishing Company.

Deere, C. D., 2005. *The feminization of agriculture? Economic restructuring in rural Latin America* (No. 1). Geneva: United Nations Research Institute for Social Development.

Degenhardt, L., Chiu, W. T., Sampson, N., Kessler, R. C., Anthony, J. C., Angermeyer, M., Bruffaerts, R., De Girolamo, G., Gureje, O., Huang, Y. and Karam, A., 2008. Toward a global view of alcohol, tobacco, cannabis, and cocaine use: Findings from the WHO World Mental Health Surveys. *PLoS Medicine, 5*(7), e141.

Desai, M. and Rinaldo, R., 2016. Reorienting gender and globalization: Introduction to the special issue. *Qualitative Sociology, 39*(4), pp.337–351.

DeVries, P., 2002. Vanishing mediators: Enjoyment as a political factor in western Mexico. *American Ethnologist, 29*(4), 901–927.

Donato, K., Gabaccia, D., Holdaway, J., Manalansan IV, M. and Pessar P., 2006. A glass half full? Gender in migration studies. *International Migration Review, 40*(1), 3–26.

Dreby, J., 2009. Gender and transnational gossip. *Qualitative Sociology, 32*(1), 33–52.

Drotbohm, H., 2010. Gossip and social control across the seas: Targeting gender, resource inequalities and support in Cape Verdean transnational families. *African and Black Diaspora: An International Journal, 3*(1), 51–68.

Duke, M. and Gómez Carpinteiro, F., 2009. The effects of problem drinking and sexual risk among Mexican migrant workers on their community of origin. *Human Organization, 68*(3), 328–339.

Dumond, D. 1997. *The machete and the cross: Campesino rebellion in Yucatán.* Lincoln: University of Nebraska Press.

Eber, C., 1995. *Women and alcohol in a highland Maya town: Water of hope, water of sorrow.* Austin: University of Texas Press.

Esteinou, R., 2005. The emergence of the nuclear family in Mexico. *International Journal of Sociology of the Family, 31*(1), 1–18.

Esteinou, R., 2007. Strengths and challenges of Mexican families in the 21st century. *Marriage & Family Review, 41*(3–4), 309–334.

Faier, L., 2011. Theorizing the intimacies of migration: Commentary on the emotional formations of transnational worlds. *International Migration, 49*(6), 107–112.

Farmer, P., 2004. An anthropology of structural violence. *Current Anthropology, 45*(3), 305–325.

Farmer, P. E., Nizeye, B., Stulac, S. and Keshavjee, S., 2006. Structural violence and clinical medicine. *PLoS Medicine, 3*(10), e449.

Ferguson, J., 1990. *The anti-politics machine: "Development," depoliticization and bureaucratic power in Lesotho.* Minneapolis: University of Minnesota Press.

Fernández-Kelly, P. and Massey, D. S., 2007. Borders for whom? The role of NAFTA in Mexico-US migration. *The Annals of the American Academy of Political and Social Science, 610*(1), 98–118.

Fitting, E., 2011. *The struggle for maize: Campesinos, workers, and transgenic corn in the Mexican countryside.* Durham: Duke University Press.

Folan Higgins, W., Domínguez Carrasco, M., Gunn, J., Morales López, A., González Heredia, R., Villanueva García, G. and Torrescano Valle, N., 2015. Calakmul: Power, Perseverance, and Persistence. In *Archaeology and bioarchaeology of population movement among the prehispanic Maya.* A. Cucina, ed. New York: Springer, pp. 37–50.

Fox, J. and Haight, N., 2010. *Subsidizing inequality: Mexican corn policy since NAFTA.* Washington, DC: Woodrow Wilson International Center for Scholars.

Frank, R. and Wildsmith, E., 2005. The grass widows of Mexico: Migration and union dissolution in a binational context. *Social Forces, 83*(3), 919–947.

Freeman, C., 2001. Is local: global as feminine: masculine? Rethinking the gender of globalization. *Signs: Journal of Women in Culture and Society, 26*(4), 1007–1037.

Gaibazzi, P., 2013. Cultivating hustlers: The agrarian ethos of Soninke migration. *Journal of Ethnic and Migration Studies, 39*(2), 259–275.

Gálvez, A., 2018. *Eating NAFTA: Trade, food policies, and the destruction of Mexico.* Berkeley: University of California Press.

Garcia, A., 2010. *The pastoral clinic: Addiction and dispossession along the Rio Grande.* Berkeley: University of California Press.

García, V., 2008. Problem drinking among transnational Mexican migrants: Exploring migrant status and situational factors. *Human Organization*, 67(1), 12–24.

Garcini, L., Peña, J., Galvan, T., Fagundes, C., Malcarne, V. and Klonoff, E., 2017. Mental disorders among undocumented Mexican immigrants in high-risk neighborhoods: Prevalence, comorbidity, and vulnerabilities. *Journal of Consulting and Clinical Psychology*, 85(10), 927–936.

Gaytán, M., 2014. Drinking difference: Race, consumption, and alcohol prohibition in Mexico and the United States. *Ethnicities*, 14(3): 436-457.

Glick Schiller, N., Basch, L. and Blanc–Szanton, C., 1992. Towards a definition of transnationalism. *Annals of the New York Academy of Sciences*, 645(1), ix–xiv.

Glick Schiller, N. and Salazar, N. B., 2013. Regimes of mobility across the globe. *Journal of Ethnic and Migration Studies*, 39(2), 183–200.

Goldberg, P., ed. 2014. *Unaccompanied children leaving Central America and Mexico and the need for international protection.* Washington, DC: United Nations High Commissioner on Refugees.

Gomberg-Muñoz, R., 2016. *Becoming legal: Immigration, law, and mixed-status families.* Oxford: Oxford University Press.

González-López, G., 2005. *Erotic journeys: Mexican immigrants and their sex lives.* Berkeley: University of California Press.

Grigolini, S., 2005. When houses provide more than shelter. In *Migration and economy: Global and local dynamics.* L. Trager, ed. Lanham: Altamira Press, pp. 193–224.

Gutmann, M. C., 1997. *The meanings of macho: Being a man in Mexico City.* Berkeley: University of California Press.

Haenn, N., 2005. *Fields of power, forests of discontent: Culture, conservation, and the state in Mexico.* Tucson: University of Arizona Press.

Haenn, N., 2016. The middle-class conservationist: Social dramas, blurred identity boundaries, and their environmental consequences in Mexican conservation. *Current Anthropology*, 57(2), 197–118.

Haenn, N., Schmook, B., Reyes Martínez, Y. and Calmé, S., 2014. Improving conservation outcomes with insights from local experts and bureaucracies. *Conservation Biology*, 28(4), 951–958.

Hannaford, D., 2017. *Marriage without borders: Transnational spouses in neoliberal Senegal.* Philadelphia: University of Pennsylvania Press.

Hart, J. M., 2002. *Empire and revolution: The Americans in Mexico since the Civil War.* Berkeley: University of California Press.

Harvey, N.,1998. *The Chiapas rebellion: The struggle for land and democracy.* Durham: Duke University Press.

Hinojosa-Ojeda, R., 2012. Economic benefits of comprehensive immigration reform. *The Cato Journal, 32,* 175.

Hirsch, J., 2003. *A courtship after marriage: Sexuality and love in Mexican transnational families.* Berkeley: University of California Press.

Hirsch, J. S., Wardlow, H., Smith, D. J., Phinney, H., Parikh, S. and Nathanson, C. A., 2009. *The secret: Love, marriage, and HIV.* Nashville: Vanderbilt University Press.

Holden, R. H., 1994. *Mexico and the survey of public lands: The management of modernization, 1876–1911.* DeKalb: Northern Illinois University Press.

Holmes, S., 2013. *Fresh fruit, broken bodies: Migrant farmworkers in the United States.* Berkeley: University of California Press.

Hondagneu-Sotelo, P. ed., 2003. *Gender and US immigration: Contemporary trends.* Berkeley: University of California Press.

Hondagneu-Sotelo, P., 1994. *Gendered transitions: Mexican experiences of immigration.* Berkeley: University of California Press.

Hsu, M. Y., 2000. *Dreaming of gold, dreaming of home: Transnationalism and migration between the United States and South China, 1882–1943.* Palo Alto: Stanford University Press.

INEGI (Instituto Nacional de Estadística y Geografía e Información). 2010. *Censo general de población y vivienda, México.* Aguascalientes: Instituto Nacional de Estadística, Geografía e Informática.

INEGI (Instituto Nacional de Estadística y Geografía e Información). 2015. *Tabulados de la Encuesta Intercensal.* Aguascalientes: Instituto Nacional de Estadística, Geografía e Informática

James, P., 2005. Arguing globalizations: Propositions towards an investigation of global formation. *Globalizations,* 2(2), 193–209.

Jimenez, M., 2009. *Humanitarian crisis: Migrant deaths at the US-Mexico border.* San Jacobo: American Civil Liberties Union of San Jacobo & Imperial Counties and Mexico's National Commission of Human Rights.

Jiménez, M. F., 1995. From plantation to cup: Coffee and capitalism in the United States, 1830–1930. In *Coffee, society, and power in Latin America.* Roseberry and Gudmundson, eds. Baltimore: Johns Hopkins University Press, pp. 38 61.

Johnson, D. 2017. The most dangerous jobs in America. *Time.* http://time. com/5074471/most-dangerous-jobs/ Accessed September 1, 2018.

Jones, G. D., 1989. *Maya resistance to Spanish rule: Time and history on a colonial frontier.* Albuquerque: University of New Mexico Press.

Jónsson, G., 2011. *Non-migrant, sedentary, immobile, or 'left behind'?* International Migration Institute (Working Paper 39). Oxford: International Migration Institute.

Krissman, F., 2005. Sin coyote ni patrón: Why the 'migrant network' fails to explain international migration. *International migration review,* 1(39), 4–44.

Kohut, A., et al. 2014. *The global divide on homosexuality: Greater acceptance in more secular affluent countries.* Washington, DC: Pew Research Center.

Latour, B., 1993. *We have never been modern.* Cambridge: Harvard University Press.

León Pinelo, A., 1958 (1639). *Relación sobre la pacificación de las provincias del Manché i Lacandón.* Madrid: Gráficas Minerva.

Levine, S. E. and Correa, C. S., 1993. *Dolor y alegría: Women and social change in urban Mexico.* Madison: University of Wisconsin Press.

Levitt, P. and Jaworsky, B. N., 2007. Transnational migration studies: Past developments and future trends. *Annual Review Sociology, 33,* 129–156.

Levitt, P. and Merry, S., 2009. Vernacularization on the ground: Local uses of global women's rights in Peru, China, India and the United States. *Global Networks, 9*(4), 441–461.

Lindquist, G., 2006. *Conjuring hope: Healing and magic in contemporary Russia.* London: Berghahn Books.

Lutz, H., 2010. Gender in the migratory process. *Journal of Ethnic and Migration Studies, 36*(10), 1647–1663.

Magnoni, A., Ardren, T. and Hutson, S., 2007. Tourism in the Mundo Maya: Inventions and (mis) representations of Maya identities and heritage. *Archaeologies, 3*(3), 353–383.

Mahler, S. J. and Pessar, P. R., 2006. Gender matters: Ethnographers bring gender from the periphery toward the core of migration studies. *International Migration Review, 40*(1), 27–63.

Maloka, T., 1997. Khomo Lia Oela: Canteens, brothels and labour migrancy in colonial Lesotho, 1900–40. *Journal of African History, 38*(01), 101–122.

Mann, C. 2006. *1491: New revelations of the Americas before Columbus.* New York: Vintage Books.

Martínez, Ó. 2014. *The Beast: Riding the rails and dodging narcos on the migrant trail.* New York: Verso.

Massey, D. S., Arango, J., Hugo, G., Kouaouci, A., Pellegrino, A. and Taylor, J. E., 1993. Theories of international migration: A review and appraisal. *Population and Development Review, 19*(3), 431–466.

Mathews, J. 2009. *Chicle: The chewing gum of the Americas, from the ancient Maya to William Wrigley.* Tucson: University of Arizona Press.

Mauss, M., 2002 (1925). *The gift: The form and reason for exchange in archaic societies.* New York: Routledge.

McBride, J. and Sergie M., 2017. *NAFTA's economic impact.* Washington, DC: Council on Foreign Relations. https://www.cfr.org/backgrounder/naftas-economic-impact Accessed December 29, 2017.

McClusky, L., 2001. *'Here, our culture is hard': Stories of domestic violence from a Mayan community in Belize.* Austin: University of Texas Press.

McEvoy, J., Petrzelka, P., Radel, C. and Schmook, B., 2012. Gendered mobility and morality in a south-eastern Mexican community: Impacts of male labour migration on the women left behind. *Mobilities, 7*(3), 369–388.

McKeown, A., 2010. Chinese emigration in global context, 1850–1940. *Journal of Global History, 5*(01), 95–124.

Menjívar, C., 2011. *Enduring violence: Ladina women's lives in Guatemala.* Berkeley: University of California Press.

Merry, S. E., 1997. Rethinking gossip and scandal. In *Reputation: Studies in the voluntary elicitation of good conduct.* Klein, ed. Ann Arbor: University of Michigan Press, pp. 47–74.

Merry, S. E., 2000. *Colonizing Hawai'i: The cultural power of law.* Princeton: Princeton University Press.

Mitchell, T. J., 2004. *Intoxicated identities: Alcohol's power in Mexican history and culture.* New York: Psychology Press.

Moran-Taylor, M. J., 2008. Guatemala's Ladino and Maya migra landscapes: The tangible and intangible outcomes of migration. *Human Organization, 67*(2), 111–124.

Nawyn, S. J., 2010. Gender and migration: Integrating feminist theory into migration studies. *Sociology Compass, 4*(9), 749–765.

Naughton-Treves, L., Holland, M. B. and Brandon, K., 2005. The role of protected areas in conserving biodiversity and sustaining local livelihoods. *Annual Review of Environment and Resources, 30,* 219–252.

Nemogá Soto, G. R., 2004. *Inter and intra-cultural variation of medicinal plant knowledge in the tropical forest of Calakmul, Mexico.* (Doctoral dissertation, University of California, Davis).

Netting, R. M., 1993. *Smallholders, householders: Farm families and the ecology of intensive, sustainable agriculture.* Palo Alto: Stanford University Press.

Newell S., 2014. The matter of the unfetish: Hoarding and the spirit of possessions. *HAU: Journal of Ethnographic Theory. 4*(3), 185–213.

Nilan, P. and Feixa, C., eds., 2006. *Global youth? Hybrid identities, plural worlds.* New York: Routledge.

Nobles, J. and McKelvey, C., 2015. Gender, power and emigration from Mexico. *Demography, 52*(5), 1573–1600.

Organisation for Economic Cooperation and Development (OECD). 2015. *OECD Employment Outlook 2015.* Paris: OECD Publishing. http://dx.doi.org/10.1787/empl_outlook-2015-en Accessed January 3, 2018.

Padilla, M. B., Hirsch, J. S. and Muñoz-Laboy, M., 2007. *Love and globalization: Transformations of intimacy in the contemporary world.* Nashville: Vanderbilt University Press.

Passel, J., Cohn, D. and González Barrera, A., 2012. *Net migration from Mexico falls to zero—and perhaps less.* Washington, DC: Pew Research Center.

Pasternak, B. and Ember, M., 1997. *Sex, gender, and kinship: A cross-cultural perspective.* New York: Pearson College Division.

Pauli, J., 2008. A house of one's own: Gender, migration, and residence in rural Mexico. *American Ethnologist, 35*(1), 171–187.

Pérez Vázquez, R., López Reyes, Y. and Avalos Placencia, T., 2013. *Historias del desplazamiento interno forzado en Tila, Chiapas (1995–2005).* Mexico City: Programa Conjunto por una Cultura de Paz.

Pérez Chacón, J., 1993 (1988). *Jiñi ch'olubü tyi Tila yik'oty imelbalob tyi pañümil/ Los Choles de Tila y su mundo.* Tuxtla Gutiérrez: Gobierno del Estado de Chiapas.

Pessar, P. R. and Mahler, S. J., 2003. Transnational migration: Bringing gender in. *International Migration Review, 37*(3), 812–846.

Piché, V., 2013. Contemporary migration theories as reflected in their founding texts. *Population, 68*(1), 141–164.

Pielke Jr., R. A., 2007. *The honest broker: Making sense of science in policy and politics.* Cambridge: Cambridge University Press.

Pine, J., 2007. Economy of speed: The new narco-capitalism. *Public Culture*, 19(2), 357–366.

Pitarch, P., 2010. *The jaguar and the priest: An ethnography of Tzeltal souls*. Austin: University of Texas Press.

Ponce Jiménez, M., 1990. *Montaña chiclera Campeche: Vida cotidiana y trabajo (1900–1950)*. Mexico City: Centro de Investigaciones y Estudios Superiores en Antropología Social.

Portes, A., 2000. Globalization from below: the rise of transnational communities. In *The ends of globalization: Bringing society back in*. Kalb et al., eds. Lanham, MD: Rowman and Littlefield, pp. 253–270.

Pratt M. L., 1992. *Imperial eyes: Travel writing and transculturation*. New York: Routledge.

Pribilsky, J., 2007. *La chulla vida: Gender, migration, and the family in Andean Ecuador and New York City*. Syracuse: Syracuse University Press.

Radel, C., Schmook, B., Haenn, N. and Green, L., 2017. The gender dynamics of conditional cash transfers and smallholder farming in Calakmul, Mexico. *Women's Studies International Forum*, 65(1), 17–27.

Reeder, L., 2003. *Widows in white: Migration and the transformation of rural Italian women, Sicily, 1880–1920*. Toronto: University of Toronto Press.

Restall, M., 2004. Maya ethnogenesis. *Journal of Latin American Anthropology*, 9(1), 64–89.

Reyes Ramos, M., 1992. *El reparto de tierras y la política agraria en Chiapas, 1914–1988*. Mexico City: Universidad Nacional Autónoma de México.

Rodman, D. H., 2006. *Gender, migration, and transnational identities: Maya and Ladino relations in eastern Guatemala* (Doctoral dissertation, University of Florida).

Rodriguez-Solorzano, C. 2014. Unintended outcomes of farmers' adaptation to climate variability: Deforestation and conservation in Calakmul and Maya biosphere reserves. *Ecology and Society*, 19(2): 53. http://dx.doi.org/10.5751/ES-06509-190253

Ruiz Nápoles, P. and Ordáz Díaz, J. L., 2011. Evolución reciente del empleo y el desempleo en México. *Journal of Economic Literature*, 8(23), 91–105.

Rus, J., 1983. Whose caste war? Indians, Ladinos and the Chiapas 'Caste War' of 1869. In *Spaniards and Indians in southeastern Mesoamerica*. MacLeod and Wasserstrom, eds. Lincoln: University of Nebraska Press, pp. 127–168.

Rus, J., 2003. Coffee and the recolonization of highland Chiapas, Mexico: Indian communities and plantation labor, 1892–1912. In *The global coffee economy in Africa, Asia, and Latin America, 1500–1989*. Clarence-Smith and Topic, eds. Cambridge: Cambridge University Press, pp. 257–285.

Sahlins, M., 2013. *What kinship is—and is not*. Chicago: University of Chicago Press.

Salazar, N. B., 2011. The power of imagination in transnational mobilities. *Identities*, 18(6), 576–598.

Salazar, N. B. and Smart, A., 2011. Anthropological takes on (im) mobility. *Identities*, 18(6), i–ix.

Samper, D., 2002. Cannibalizing kids: Rumor and resistance in Latin America. *Journal of Folklore Research, 39*(1), 1–32.

Schmook, B., Haenn, N., Radel, C. and Navarro-Olmedo, S., 2018. Empowering women? Conditional cash transfers and the patriarchal state in Calakmul, Mexico. In *Money from the government in Latin America: Social cash transfer policies and rural lives*. Balen and Fotta, eds. New York: Routledge Press, pp. 97-113.

Schmook, B. and Radel, C., 2008. International labor migration from a tropical development frontier: Globalizing households and an incipient forest transition. *Human Ecology, 36*(6), 891–908.

Schwartz, N. 1990. *Forest society: A social history of Petén, Guatemala.* Philadelphia: University Pennsylvania Press.

Sharpe, P. ed., 2002. *Women, gender and labour migration: Historical and cultural perspectives.* London: Routledge.

Simmel, G. 1950. *The sociology of Georg Simmel.* K. Wolff, ed. New York: Free Press.

Skolnik, J., Lazo de la Vega, S. and Steigenga, T., 2012. *Chisme* across borders: The impact of gossip in a Guatemalan transnational community. *Migraciones Internacionales, 6*(3), 9–38.

Stephen, L., 2007. *Transborder lives: Indigenous Oaxacans in Mexico, California, and Oregon.* Durham: Duke University Press.

Striffler, S., 2007. Neither here nor there: Mexican immigrant workers and the search for home. *American Ethnologist, 34*(4), 674–688.

Stross, B., 1974. Tzeltal marriage by capture. *Anthropological Quarterly, 47*(3), 328–346.

Thornton, J., 1998. *Africa and Africans in the making of the Atlantic World, 1400-1800.* Cambridge: Cambridge University Press.

Toledo Tello, S., 2002. *Fincas, poder y cultura en Simojovel, Chiapas.* Mexico City: Universidad Nacional Autónoma de México.

Tsing, A. L., 2005. *Friction: An ethnography of global connection.* Princeton: Princeton University Press.

Tsuda, T., Tapias, M. and Escandell, X., 2014. Locating the global in transnational ethnography. *Journal of Contemporary Ethnography, 43*(2), 123–147.

Tucker, C. M., 2011. *Coffee culture: Local experiences, global connections.* London: Routledge.

Turner, V. 1982. *From ritual to theatre: The human seriousness of play.* New York: PAJ Publications.

United States Bureau of Labor Statistics. 2016. *Databases, tables, and calculators by subject.* https://www.bls.gov/data/. Accessed January 3, 2018.

United States Bureau of Labor Statistics. 2016. Construction laborers and helpers. https://www.bls.gov/ooh/construction-and-extraction/construction-laborers-and-helpers.htm#tab-6. Accessed September 4, 2018.

United States Department of State. 2016. *Report of the visa office 2016.* https://travel.state.gov/content/travel/en/legal/visa-law0/visa-statistics/annual-reports/report-of-the-visa-office-2016.html. Accessed September 4, 2018.

Vidal Angles, C., Esquivel Campos, A., Saucedo Villegas, J., Dominguez Turriza, M., eds. *Blanco y negro: Calakmul imágenes.* Campeche: Centro INAH Campeche, Instituto de Cultura de Campeche, and Universidad Autónoma de Campeche.

Vogt, W. A., 2013. Crossing Mexico: Structural violence and the commodification of undocumented Central American migrants. *American Ethnologist,* 40(4), 764–780.

Walker, L., 2013. *Waking from the dream: Mexico's middle classes after 1968.* Palo Alto: Stanford University Press.

Weisbrot, M., Lefebvre, S. and Sammut, J., 2014. *Did NAFTA help Mexico? An assessment after 20 years* (No. 2014-03). Washington, DC: Center for Economic and Policy Research (CEPR).

West, P. 2008 Tourism as science and science as tourism: Environment, society, self, and other in Papua New Guinea. *Current Anthropology,* 49(4), 597–626.

Wilk, R. R., 1991. *Household ecology: Economic change and domestic life among the Kekchi Maya in Belize.* Tucson: University of Arizona Press.

Wilk, R. R. and Cliggett, L., 2007. *Economies and cultures: Foundations of Economic Anthropology.* Boulder: Westview Press.

Winters, A., 2014. Mexico and expropriation: The case of the German-American Coffee Company. *Anthós,* 6(1), 237–259.

Wise, T. 2010. The impacts of US agricultural policies on Mexican producers. In *Subsidizing inequality: Mexican corn policy since NAFTA.* Fox and Haight, eds. Washington, DC: Woodrow Wilson International Center for Scholars, pp. 163–172.

Wolf, E. R., 1982. *Europe and the people without history.* Berkeley: University of California Press.

Womack, J. 1999. *Rebellion in Chiapas: An historical reader.* New York: New Press.

Worby, P. A. and Organista, K. C., 2007. Alcohol use and problem drinking among male Mexican and Central American im/migrant laborers: A review of the literature. *Hispanic Journal of Behavioral Sciences,* 29(4), 413–455.

Yabiku, S. T., Agadjanian, V. and Sevoyan, A., 2010. Husbands' labour migration and wives' autonomy, Mozambique 2000–2006. *Population Studies,* 64(3), 293–306.

Zahniser, S. and Coyle, W. T., 2004. *US-Mexico corn trade during the NAFTA era: New twists to an old story.* Washington: DC: US Department of Agriculture.

Zavella, P., 2011. *I'm neither here nor there: Mexicans' quotidian struggles with migration and poverty.* Durham: Duke University Press.

INDEX

....